HAUNTED HOUSES
FOR THE MILLIONS

HAUNTED HOUSES
FOR THE MILLIONS

by Susy Smith

Bell Publishing Company, Inc. • New York

Contents

CHAPTER ONE

Introduction

Anybody who laughs at haunted houses has never been in one on a dark night. Every town has one or two old homes which have been allowed to deteriorate and which then get the reputation for being haunted. Very likely most of them are not actually ghost infested, or if they are, their ghosts are not very interesting ones. Anyone passing the night in them would probably experience more from his own imagination than from any actual spookiness inherent in the house. For, yes, I'm going to admit from the outset that, while many ghosts are genuine, authentic, and highly interesting, others are invented or imagined, and many are quite definitely hallucinated.

The great Dr. Samuel Johnson, who is best known for his dictionary and for James Boswell's biography of his life, has made a very astute statement about ghosts which holds as much sound solid sense today as it did in 1770. Dr. Johnson said:

"I make a distinction between what a man may experience by the mere strength of his imagination, and what imagination cannot possibly produce. Thus, suppose I should think I saw a form and heard a voice cry, 'Johnson, you are very wicked—and unless you repent, you will

7

certainly be punished'; my own unworthiness is so deeply impressed on my mind, that I might imagine I thus saw and heard, and therefore I should not believe that an external communication had been made to me. But if a form should appear and a spectral voice should tell me that a particular man had died at a particular place and at a particular hour—a fact which I had no apprehension of, nor any means of knowing, and this fact, with all its circumstances, should afterwards be unquestionably proved; I should in that case be persuaded that I had supernatural intelligence imparted to me."

There are many historical instances in which ghosts have obviously come back for a specific purpose. These don't haunt houses, however; they make their appearance, impart their supernatural intelligence, and depart, to be heard from no more. The most famous of all these is an old gentleman named Chaffin, who splendidly illustrates my point.

James Chaffin of Davie County, North Carolina, died in 1921, leaving a will which cut out his wife and all his sons except Marshall. One night in 1925, his son James saw his father's ghost and received a message from him. James testified in court as follows: "On a night during the latter part of June, 1925, my father appeared at my bedside, dressed as I had often seen him in life, in a familiar black overcoat. He took hold of the coat, pulled it back, and said, 'You will find my will in my overcoat pocket.' Then he disappeared."

James tracked the overcoat to the home of his brother John. He found an inner pocket stitched up, cut the stitches, and discovered inside not the actual will itself but a piece of paper on which were the words, "Read the 27th

Chapter of Genesis in my daddie's old Bible." Taking his daughter and two neighbors as witnesses, James Chaffin, Jr., went to his mother's house, found the old Bible, and looked up the Genesis chapter. Folded between the pages was a will in his father's handwriting which invalidated the previous one, divided the property equally among all four sons, and added, "You must all take care of your Mammy." This will was admitted to probate in the State of North Carolina.

On occasion a ghost will appear in order to tell someone he is dead. A young man much enamored of Mrs. Emily Clark of Newcastle-on-Tyne, England, did just this. While feeding her baby, Mrs. Clark felt a cold draft, looked up, and saw this chap standing there gazing at her with a sad expression on his face. She later learned that the garb in which he appeared to her was that which he had worn when he died from an overdose of sleeping tablets. She was never able to rid herself of the feeling that he had killed himself in grief because she had married someone else.

To give a return engagement more authenticity, it is helpful if the main character in the drama can allow himself to be seen by as many persons as possible. Samuel Bull, a chimney sweep who died in June, 1931, did just this. In February, 1932, his daughter, Mrs. Edwards, saw her father ascend the stairs and pass through a closed door into the room, then unused, in which he had died. Almost immediately afterwards his grandson, James Hull, age twenty-one, also saw him. Later all the members of the family, including Mrs. Edwards' five children, together observed him. At that time the little five-year-old girl cried out to "Grandpa Bull." The apparition continued to appear at frequent intervals until about April 9th. It is not known whether or not he had any important news to impart other than that it was possible for him to survive death and to make his ghost appear. This, it would seem, would be an effort momentous enough to be worthy of any deceased entity's time.

Another alleged spirit who was seen by a number of people, managing to appear frequently for over a year, is the first American ghost about whom any documentary evidence exists: Mrs. Nelly Butler. She made herself evident initially as a voice from out of nowhere in the home of Abner Blaisdel, on the coast near Machiasport, Maine, on the night of August 9, 1799. She returned again on January 2, 1800, and at that time she said she was the deceased wife of Captain George Butler, had been David Hooper's daughter Nelly, and that she was soon going to be able to show herself as an apparition. This she accomplished one day late in January, and she was able to keep it up intermittently for a number of months. While seen by as many as one hundred people during this time, and recognized by those who had known her, she also brought evidence of her identity in the things she said, and she showed an ability to predict events which later came true. She used Abner Blaisdel's cellar as her headquarters and frequently appeared there as a glowing, beautiful spirit before one or two individuals or when there were as many as fifty people gathered to see her. She was quite a ham, loved an audience, and made the most of it.

The Reverend Abraham Cummings, a well-educated man who was a graduate of Brown University, was firmly convinced that the members of his congregation who were claiming to have seen the ghost of Mrs. Butler had flipped their lids—until he saw her himself. He was walking across an open field one day when suddenly he saw ahead of him a globe of light with a rosy tinge. He turned directly toward the amazing spectacle so that he could examine it closely, keeping his eyes fixed intently on it for fear it might disappear. But he had not gone more than five paces when the glowing mass flashed right to where he was and instantly resolved itself into the shape of a woman. It was small, however—the size of a child of seven. Staring at it in amazement, the parson thought, "You're not tall enough for the woman who has been appearing among us." Immediately, the figure expanded to normal size, and now, he wrote afterwards, "she appeared glorious," with rays of light shining from her head all about and reaching to the ground. As he gazed at the vision, the Reverend Mr. Cummings was filled with two strangely conflicting emotions. One, he says, was genuine fright. "But," he adds in his account of his experience, "my fear was connected with ineffable pleasure."

In another moment the Spectre, as she was always called, was gone, but the influence of that radiant apparition never left Cummings for the rest of his life. After that, he says, all mundane things seemed dull and commonplace and of no real value.

The reason Mrs. Butler appeared, she said, was because she wanted to make sure her husband married Lydia Blaisdel. The fact that they were already courting, and that being championed by a ghost only made Lydia suspect for trying to get a husband the hard way, actually made matters worse for all concerned. As soon as the marriage was consummated, Nelly whispered in Captain Butler's ear that he must be kind to Lydia because she would die in childbirth within a year's time; and this prediction came to pass. We can't help but wonder, somehow, why the ghost meddled, and if she was really trying to be as helpful as she maintained.

Anyway, Abraham Cummings was to revere her forever as the best evidence ever received for the continuity of conscious life after death. He made it his goal from then on to pass along the word of this great miracle in which he had participated. He fortunately had the presence of mind to assemble many trustworthy witnesses who wrote out and signed their statements about what they had seen and what they had heard when Nelly Butler appeared. He then published them in a pamphlet for "the testimony of the sense to the truth of the belief in immortality." The pamphlet appeared in 1826, the year before Cummings died, and a copy of it exists today at Brown University. Another edition was issued in Portland as late as 1859, and of it there are, so far as is known, three copies extant.

So, as these examples indicate, there is evidence that ghosts can appear for specific reasons and can make their reasons known. But it is not apparitions of this kind which actually haunt houses. Hauntings rarely seem to indicate purpose. A haunt may reveal his identity by the fact that he looks like a certain deceased person, or that he repeats a certain ritual previously performed by that individual. But even in these cases the entity's conscious intent to appear is seldom evident. The apparition usually seems to be in a dreamlike state and its activities are mechanical—as if they were a subconscious repetition of former events or emotional crises. These ghosts could be explained as "earthbound spirits" who wish to continue to live their lives as they did while on earth, perhaps not even realizing that they have died, or if so, not knowing what to do about it.

An excellent example of this type of ghost is Ann Mary Macy, who lived in a yellow cottage on a little hill in Siasconset, Nantucket Island, off the coast of Massachusetts. A prominent writer was living in Nantucket one summer with her husband and their six-months-old baby and her nurse. The writer was trying in her spare time to compose adequate prose, but found she had no room even to think in the small house in which they lived. When she complained of this to her friend Frederick Howe, one-time Commissioner of Immigration for the Port of New York, he loaned her his cottage as a writing office every afternoon while he was on the golf course. There she was able to write peacefully, but occasionally while pausing and walking around the room in which she worked she would find herself unconsciously rearranging the furniture a little bit, pushing a chair or two around at some different angle. Of course, she always changed it back again before she left. One rocking chair particularly she always found herself pulling over in front of a certain window. Being psychic, this writer, after a few days, began to realize that someone invisible was sitting in that rocking chair. She was quite comfortable with this pleasant visitor, and even learned to have a feeling of companionship.

Finally, one day when she was holding a pen loosely in her hand in an effort to do automatic writing with her deceased brother, the visiting author found that her pen had written the name "Ann Mary Macy." When she allowed this correspondent to continue, she learned that Ann Mary Macy had lived and died in that house. Mrs. Macy wrote that she had been encouraging the writer to move the furniture back the way she had preferred it. She later wrote via typewriter the story of her life: Her husband, John Macy, had stolen money from the bank where he worked and speculated on the market with it. When the bank examiners came, he ran away; and she remained there to raise their son Johnny alone. When Johnny was seven the children at school began to tease him about his father, so she sent him away to be raised by relatives to keep him from learning of his family disgrace. She lived on alone there, and sat in her rocker many unhappy nights missing her husband and child and thinking about the good life they once had there together. One day years later she died in her rocking chair by the window. Now she was telling her story—and as evidence she gave the names of local people who could verify it. When the woman writer checked with those mentioned, she found that this entire account, previously unknown to her, was true.

Poor little Ann Mary Macy was obviously an earthbound spirit, still monotonously living her lonely life, not realizing that there was more for her in the hereafter than there had been in her worldly experience.

Aside from ghosts with a purpose, and ghosts without a purpose, there is another brand of spook which is actually much more prevalent. And this is what haunts more houses than anything else. It does not seem to be any kind of a remnant of an actual entity's personal consciousness. It seems rather to be more like a memory image of the person, as if some startling or highly dramatic event had left such an impact that the house was impregnated with it. The theory is: during acts of violence great waves of hysteria or emotion-laden thought are released, which somehow seem to photograph the actual event just as if a movie had been taken at the scene. This "psychic film" is capable of being seen when conditions are just right, or by especially sensitive people. It is in a way possible to regard the haunted house as a sort of storage battery of psychical force, impressed by the thoughts or memories of certain deceased individuals or of certain highly dramatic scenes.

There are also the poltergeists—those curious phenomena which cause physical activity like flying objects and bumping noises and sudden unexplained fires to occur in a house. They usually center around one person, which quite frequently, but not necessarily always, is a child in puberty. There are various theories about what causes poltergeists—from "psychokinetic force" instigated by the subconscious mind of the individual being pestered, to "the actual conscious activity of the spirits of deceased persons endeavoring to make their presence known." Some people will tell you that poltergeists are malevolent entities of some kind—whether human or devils they do not know. It is true that this kind of haunting usually does show some highly unfriendly characteristics.

Poltergeists occur quite frequently all over the world. No one knows definitely how to account for them any more than we know definitely how to account for any other kind of haunts. But we know for a fact that all the different kinds of ghostly activity I've mentioned do happen, and they have been witnessed and carefully reported by many reliable, conscientious people. Of course, it helps if you are what is known as "psychic"—more sensitive than others to supernormal impressions. Not everyone can see ghosts. Even when a whole roomfull of people are witnessing ghastly ghostly

15

goings-on, one stolid person is likely to sit there seeing and hearing nothing whatever of the manifestations. He, of course, thinks everyone else is either crazy or "seeing things."

Perhaps, instead, it is the man who *can't* see ghosts who is having the hallucination—the hallucination that everything in this world is solid and material and matter-of-fact and routine. Those who have ghostly experiences—and there are a fantastic number of us—know that the world, instead, is filled with curious psychical phenomena which challenge every iota of our intellect and ingenuity to explain. And thus every haunted house is a Pandora's box of potential excitement.

Luckily, even if you can't see ghosts, you can read about them. So read now of a great many of the interesting haunted houses of the world. Read—and enjoy!

CHAPTER TWO

Haunted English Houses

In the stately old mansions of England ghosts are a cherished tradition. So, naturally, we are likely to find many of our best stories there. The English characteristic of calm appraisal of a difficult situation has provided us with some straightforward and unemotional accounts of even the most harrowing hauntings. As long ago as 1765, Mrs. William Henry Ricketts, whose reputation for veracity was such that it was worthy of note, described the manifestations at Hinton Ampner in a most restrained fashion; but what she experienced must have, to coin a phrase, chilled the very marrow of her bones.

Hinton Ampner, which lay between Alresford and Winchester, in Hampshire, England, was probably built by Sir Thomas Stewkley sometime before 1623. It was not particularly large as manor houses went in those days; but what it lacked in size it made up in activity in later years when the ghosts arrived.

The commotion all started some time after the big scandal. The house had been inherited by a descendant of Sir Thomas, Mary Stewkley, who married Edward Stawell. Mary's younger sister, Honoria, lived with them. When his father died, Edward became Lord Stawell. Soon after, Mary died. It was against the law in those days for a man to marry his deceased wife's sister, but no one so much as winked an eye if they lived together. So Honoria continued to live with her brother-in-law, apparently in more ways than one. There were, however, certain things frowned upon by society, even then, and when Honoria was reputed to have had an illegitimate child the scandal broke out. It got worse when it was rumored that the baby had been done away with. Eventually, however, both Edward and Honoria died. That's the best way to end any kind of gossip.

Hinton Ampner Manor remained unoccupied, except for a few servants, for many years. In January, 1765, it was rented by William Henry Ricketts, a man whose business took him frequently to the West Indies. His wife, Mary, who was from a very distinguished family, mistakenly thought that this house would be just a darling place for her and their three children to remain safe and snug while her husband was away on his business trips. She had brought her servants with her from London, and, being strangers to the area, they were all just as naïve as she was about the reputation of the house.

For the first couple years that the Ricketts lived there things weren't so bad, although almost immediately the slamming of doors was heard frequently. No doors were ever found unlocked so that they could legitimately have slammed, and the banging didn't cease even when new sets of locks were put on.

Then one of the servants saw a gentleman in drab where no gentleman in drab could normally have been. When he told it around in the village he learned that a groom had also seen this same apparition ten years previously. Townspeople thought it was the ghost of naughty Lord Stawell. The same figure was seen again in the great hall one night by George Turner, Mrs. Ricketts' groom.

In July, 1767, a woman was observed dressed in dark clothes which rustled as if made of very stiff silk. Since no woman who answered that description lived in the house, certain questions began to be asked among the servants. Questions like, "What kind of a place is this, anyway?" The questions got worse as the ghosts became more active, for soon everyone in the house was hearing groans and bangings and rustlings and flutterings and whisperings.

At a time like this William Henry Ricketts took off for Jamaica, leaving his wife and children at home. Well, he had to go, of course. Business was business even in 1769. A modern psychologist would probably tell Mary that the reason she then began to hear mens' footsteps in her bedroom was Freudian. She knew better. But she *was* tempted to think that perhaps her erstwhile dependable servants were playing tricks on her. So she began to change bedrooms frequently, and usually on such sudden notice that none of the servants would have any idea in which room she was sleeping. But her invisible visitor knew, and footsteps and knockings and rappings and tappings accompanied her.

Many years after this adventure at Hinton Ampner, Mary wrote an account of her experiences for the edification of her children. She said in it: "From this time I determined to have my woman lie in a little bed in my room. The noises grew more frequent, and she was always sensible of the same sounds, and much in the same direction as they struck me. Harassed and perplexed, I was yet very unwilling to divulge my embarrassment. I had taken every method to investigate the cause, and could not discover the least appearance of a trick; on the contrary, I became convinced it was beyond the power of any mortal agent to perform, but knowing how explosive such opinions were, I kept them in my own bosom, and hoped my resolution would enable me to support whatever might befall.

"After Midsummer the noises became every night more intolerable. They began before I went to bed, and with intermissions were heard till after broad day in the morning. I could frequently distinguish articulate sounds, and usually a shrill female voice would begin, and then two others with deeper and manlike tone seemed to join in the discourse, yet, though this conversation sounded as if close to me, I never could distinguish words."

Mary managed to retain her composure and her silent tongue even when her brother came to visit her, for she didn't want to disturb him with her story. "But," she writes, "the morning after he left me to return to Portsmouth, about three o'clock and daylight, Elizabeth Godin and myself both awoke—she had been sitting up in bed looking round her, expecting as she always did to see something terrible—I heard with infinite astonishment the most loud, deep, tremendous noise which seemed to rush and fall with infinite velocity and force on the lobby floor adjoining my room. I started up and called to Godin, 'Good God! did you hear that noise?' She made no reply; on repeating the question she answered with a faltering voice. She was so frightened she scarce durst speak. Just at that instant we heard a shrill and dreadful shriek, seeming to proceed from under the spot where the rushing noise fell, and repeated three or four times, growing fainter as it seemed to descend, till it sank into earth. Hannah Streeter, who lay in the room with my children, heard the same noises, and was so appalled she lay for two hours almost deprived of sense and motion."

Well, keeping quiet about a thing like that gets to be almost silly, and so when her brother came soon again to visit, Mrs. Ricketts told him her experiences. He and a friend sat up most nights after that. They heard many of the same disturbances, and thus verified the reports that Mary and the servants had given. But even men of distinction could not account for the cause, and nothing they did seemed to halt the manifestations in any way. Mary's brother had to return home, and he refused to allow her to stay there alone. She was probably most grateful for a strong, manly decision that she should leave Hinton Ampner. She moved out, bag and baggage, children and servants, in record time.

Hinton Ampner was rented several times again, but new tenants were unable to stay there either. So eventually the house was pulled down. During its demolition the house-breakers made a curious discovery. Under the floor of one of the rooms was found a small skull. To be polite, word was given out that it was the skull of a monkey. But who could say that it didn't really belong to a human baby? It was never put before a regular inquiry and so no professional opinion was ever given as to its actual nature.

A new house was built on the same property near the foundations of the old manor, and some frightening noises have been heard there also. Even as recently as October, 1941, occupants of this new building at Hinton Ampner were still being disturbed.

The talk of London during the long-ago reign of King Charles I (1625–1649) was a house which no longer exists; but it was famous enough in its day still to be remembered for its macabre story of love, intrigue, tragedy, death, and . . . ghosts.

Cashio Burroughs, son of the English envoy to the German Emperor, was studying Italian in Florence when he fell in love with the beautiful mistress of the Grand Duke and was soon deeply involved with her. She found herself unable to be true to her mentor, because young Cashio so enraptured her heart. Unfortunately, the affair reached the ears of the Duke. (You couldn't get by with anything in those days in Italy without somebody blabbing to the authorities.) The Duke decided that perhaps the most adroit way out of the mess would be to have the young man murdered. His body could then be dropped into the River Arno and nobody would be any the wiser as to what had really happened to him.

Cashio received warning in time. (Somebody was always blabbing to the lesser lights as well.) He left Florence with such haste that he quite forgot to tell his love of his departure. It was only when she was later reproached by the Grand Duke for her treachery to him that she discovered that Cashio had deserted her. Much more involved affectionwise than her young lover had been, the heroine of this tale killed herself.

At the very moment of her death Cashio, who had naturally run home to papa and mama for safety from the wicked Grand Duke, was in his bedroom in the London house which was afterwards to become so haunted. Suddenly his ex-girlfriend's ghost appeared to him and gave him hell for abandoning her to the vengeance of the

Duke. She then warned him that he, too, would soon die—in a duel. From that time onward Cashio Burroughs was under constant assault from the dramatic Italian ghost. She returned night after night to reproach him and eventually he was so terrified he was almost crazed. He was not alone in seeing her, for other members of his family were his witnesses that things around there were definitely not like they used to be before he went off to Italy and took up with foreign women. Soon the phantom was the talk of London, and even King Charles became interested. He was a man for evidence. He wanted facts. So he sent off to Florence for confirmation of the story, and it was discovered all to be true. He also learned that the first appearance of the ghost *had* actually corresponded with the hour of the lady's demise.

The sequel is that she wasn't just good at making her phantom appear, she was also just loaded with ESP. Cashio was killed in a duel within the time she had stipulated.

Today the Borley Rectory is a shell, standing and staring at the world with vacant-window eyes. But before it was gutted by fire in 1939, it was known as the most haunted house in England. Near Sudbury, Suffolk, it was a large, rambling, uncomfortable, and inconvenient house which had been built by the Reverend Henry Bull in 1863. Since he had a family of seventeen children, Bull needed more space, and so in 1875 he added a new wing which converted the structure into a rectangular building almost completely enclosing a bricked courtyard. It then had thirty-five rooms, and every one of them was haunted.

Nearly every type of ghostly phenomenon has been

experienced there. Many figures were seen, including a nun, Henry Bull's son Harry (after his death), a headless man, a figure in gray, a girl in white, and other shadowy forms. Also seen and heard quite often was a ghostly coach-and-four, the rumbling of the coach and the galloping of the horses having swept down the much-too-narrow lane hundreds of times.

These phenomena were experienced at the Borley Rectory during Bull's lifetime and by subsequent churchmen who inhabited the house, as well as by the villagers. Then there were the many scientists and medical men, university students, consulting engineers, army officers, and R.A.F. pilots who came to investigate over the years—many of them witnessed or heard things, too. Among the most obvious noises, besides the galloping horses, were a woman's voice, whisperings, a dog padding around the room, scratchings, incessant bell-ringing, footsteps, raps, taps, clicks and cracks, bumps and thumps, doors closing, jumping and stamping, the sound of rushing water, crashes as of falling crockery, the smashing of windows, and church music.

Wall writing appeared in rooms which were under control. That means that the room was sealed up and honest guards stationed at all the doors and windows—and still the phenomenon would appear inside. The writing was usually a pathetic plea for help, but no one knew who it was that needed help or what to do about it. Whether the fact that the building had been erected on the foundations of an older rectory on the same site has anything to do with it is questionable. There is also a persistent tradition that a monastery once occupied the site, but no concrete evidence of this exists. So no one really ever knew what was back of it all.

The Reverend G. Eric Smith, a later tenant, heard whisperings often, and one dusk when he crossed the landing he heard a woman's voice, half moan and half appeal, say loudly, "Don't, Carlos, don't." To my knowledge there was never a clergyman named Carlos who lived in the house. This fact must have mollified the Reverend Mr. Smith somewhat.

That coach-and-four, or actually, coach-and-pair, as it was most often observed, was one of the most interesting manifestations at Borley. A man named Edward Cooper, who was combination groom and gardener for the Bull family, saw it several times—a phantom coach-and-pair, brilliantly lit up and glittering in the moonlight, silently racing across the church meadows, through trees, walls, and hedges, and finally disappearing in the farmyard below.

The Reverend Harry Bull, who succeeded his father as rector, also saw it. He always maintained that he had personal communications with the spirits in that house. He insisted that if he was discontented after death, and was able to do so, he would return and cause some kind of violent physical manifestations there, such as smashing glass or some other noisy demonstration. Actually, after his death his ghost was seen on several occasions by the wife of the Reverend L. A. Foyster, the rector who succeeded him.

Things got very exciting there during Mr. Foyster's term; and psychical researcher Harry Price heard about it and decided to investigate. He rented the house for a year and observed the ghostly capers constantly, along with friends and other researchers who visited him. He writes in *Poltergeist over England*: "On May 9, 1938, I gave up the tenancy of the Rectory. My experiment had been brilliantly successful. Nearly every type of phenomenon experienced at Borley was repeated, *under scientific conditions,* and recorded by disinterested and dispassionate witnesses."

Of course, there are those psychical researchers who maintain that Harry Price manufactured some of the evidence himself—but there are those in this field who will say anything, if it is vindictive enough, against others.

Captain W. H. Gregson bought the Rectory at the end of 1938, and his dogs added some new phenomena to the old ones which he witnessed. He lost in succession two valuable spaniel puppies. Both reacted in the same way—each, on separate occasions, followed him into the courtyard when he heard footsteps and went to investigate. Then, he says, "the dog stopped dead, and positively went mad. He shrieked and tore away, still shrieking." Neither dog has been seen since.

It was while Captain Gregson owned the Rectory that it caught fire. A paraffin lamp fell over of its own accord. While the house burned a local policeman testified that he saw a woman in gray and a man wearing a bowler hat in front of Captain Gregson as he walked about the courtyard at two o'clock in the morning, even though no such persons actually were present. Those who have visited the Rectory ruins by moonlight have seen a young woman dressed in pale blue or white suddenly appear at the Blue Room window—but since just the shell of the building remains and there are neither floor nor interior walls to the Blue Room, no human being could have been standing there.

Moyles Court is a picturesque old Manor House in the New Forest, in Ringwood, Hampshire. The original

26

manor was known to exist in 1086, and that's quite a long time ago. Today the building is used as a school for girls, who say they would like to see the haunt and would make her most welcome—but it was a stranger who had the most interesting encounter with her recently.

Lilian Chapman was there by chance with friends in September, 1962, when the building was for sale. She says: "As we drove through the double iron gates over the gravel sweep of drive to the rear entrance, the old brick house with its enormous chimney stacks was bathed in sunshine which almost made us ignore the sad state of repair the house and garden were in."

They obtained the key from the caretaker and wandered from room to room; but when her friends went to inspect the second floor Mrs. Chapman decided to wait for them in the sun which streamed in through the leaded window on the landing. She says she seated herself on the window sill and began to daydream about the families who had occupied this old house through the long centuries, wondering if they had been happy. She felt not all of them had been, "because as I waited I seemed to be overcome with a feeling of fear and sadness."

As Mrs. Chapman looked toward the doors which led to the Minstrel's Gallery, she was amazed to see, coming through them, a shadowy figure in a drab yellow cloak. There seemed more cloak than figure. The small cape piece nearly covered a pair of hands which were clasped in anguish or prayer. The hands clasped and unclasped as the apparition approached Mrs. Chapman, who says she felt no fear, only an intense sorrow. "And I swear I heard a gentle sigh as the figure passed me and drifted to the end of the landing. From there it returned to go down the stairs, seeming to disappear through a window facing the chapel."

Mrs. Chapman later inquired if there was a ghost in this house. There was—the famous "Lady in Yellow" who had haunted it ever since about 1685. She apparently had something special to do with the hall window, for it was never possible to keep it closed. It was always found open no matter how securely it had been locked. The fact that Mrs. Chapman had not been briefed in advance, and that the woman in yellow she had seen had disappeared through this very window, gives considerable weight to her story.

She learned that her apparition was known to be Alice, Lady Lisle, who had been charged with high treason because she gave shelter for the night at Moyles Court to two fugitives from the Battle of Sedgemoor—the Reverend John Hicks, a dissenting minister, and Richard Nelthorpe, a London lawyer. Lady Lisle, who may have had Puritan sympathies at a time when they were unpopular, was railroaded into prison. Her trial was a travesty, and she was allowed no lawyer for her defense. Many influential people pleaded with the king to spare the old lady's life, but he would not go beyond substituting beheading in place of burning.

And so Lady Lisle met her death with gallantry. Does she, unfortunately, still relive the days of her anguish? Or did her great travail make some kind of a memory image which still remains in the atmosphere of her home? Won't it be exciting when the time comes that we really learn scientifically exactly what it is that causes such hauntings?

An English home with quite a shady reputation is the Ash Manor House in Sussex. A mediaeval gem in a pastoral setting, it was originally built in the time of Edward the Confessor. Part of the original thirteenth century structure, having seen centuries of bloodshed and many disastrous fires, still stands. The rest has been rebuilt after every fire.

On June 28, 1934, a new owner moved in, a hard-headed, stubborn materialist, according to Dr. Nandor Fodor who investigated the case. Fodor gives him the name "Keel" in his book *The Haunted Mind*. Keel's wife, half Russian and half British, was charming, and appeared to be unusually intelligent. The rest of the family consisted of a sixteen-year-old daughter, who was nervous and jealous of the attention paid to her mother, and a son in boarding school.

The late Dr. Fodor was a psychoanalyst, and so I might as well warn you that he thinks people who live in ghost houses usually have problems which bring on the manifestations. His analysis of the reasons behind this haunting are especially interesting.

But let's hear what happened. First we have Mr. Keel's report that there were various stampings and rappings heard by the household and servants for a period of time. Then on the night of November 18, 1934, the owner was awakened by three violent bangs on his door. His wife also heard it; and they both heard it repeated the next night. Then Mr. Keel was called away on business, and while he was gone all was quiet. When he returned, he reported to Dr. Fodor: "The room was unnaturally cold and there was something unpleasant about it. I therefore decided to remain awake and see what I could see. Nothing happened until three A.M. Then I fell asleep. A short while later I was aroused by a violent bang on the door which I had left open. I sat up with a jerk.

"Standing in the doorway I saw a little oldish man, dressed in a green smock, very muddy breeches and gaiters, a slouch hat on his head, and a handkerchief around his neck.

"I thought that a servant had left a door open and a tramp had walked in. I challenged him but got no reply. I demanded again what he wanted in my house, and, as he just stood stupidly staring at me, I jumped out of bed and seized him by the shoulder. My hand went right through him. I lost my balance and must have fainted from the shock.

"All that I remember is that eventually I reached my wife's bedroom and babbled so incoherently that she ran back along the passage to get some brandy."

As Mrs. Keel reports it, her husband ran into her room and collapsed in a dead faint. Running down the hall to get him something to stimulate him, she also saw the ghost, which she mistook for a tramp. She says, "His face was very red, the eyes malevolent and horrid, the mouth open and dribbling. He stared at me with the look of an idiot."

After that, "We saw the green man altogether about two dozen times." But they heard him more often. A priest came to bless the house but that only made things worse. She says, "For two nights I knelt outside my door praying and fighting some intangible force of evil. I have never been so frightened in my life. It was as if some invisible power tried to hypnotize me. I felt enclosed from every side by evil and almost succumbed."

Well, as you can see, these people were just about on the point of collapse when Dr. Fodor arrived. They told him that if he couldn't get rid of the ghost they would have to sell the house even if it meant financial ruin for them. Fodor went into action immediately. First he asked the famous medium Mrs. Eileen J. Garrett to come to the house and she went into trance there. Her control Uvani explained that in the early part of the fifteenth century there was a temporary jail for prisoners of state about five hundred yards to the west of the Ash Manor House. "Many men and women lost their lives there. There are dozens of unhappy souls about. If a particular one comes to trouble you it is because that one has an affinity with you. If you are nervously depleted and live in this room, you give out energy with which the ghost builds itself up like a picture on the stage."

After this the entity itself was allowed to possess the medium. At first he could not speak, and when he finally got his voice he pled for mercy. Using mediaeval diction he told a long story about being a prisoner, then tortured and murdered. He wished to wreak vengeance on "Buckingham" for betraying him.

This concept that the ghost might be a spectral automaton, living on life he borrowed from the human wrecks who lived in the house, is damaging to the owners. But Dr. Fodor learned that the family situation was bad enough to attract just such an entity. He discovered that "The woman lacked sexual fulfillment. Her husband was a homosexual. The relationship between them was strained." Then Mrs. Keel had begun to take drugs. Fodor says: "On understanding this, I had tremendous sympathy for her position, and I realized how the ghost had been used as a distracting element, a sort of tranquilizer, which helped to hold the family together without bringing their true frustrations out into the open."

After these people realized the situation and faced up to their problems, their ghost went away. It has not been learned whether subsequent residents of Ash Manor have experienced any haunting, but since the publication of Fodor's account they certainly would never admit it if they had.

We couldn't possibly leave Merrie Olde England without at least one haunted hangout of the nobility. And so I give you herewith Sandringham Castle—the great country house in Norfolk where the royal family spends many of its vacations. The servants' quarters at Sandringham are consistently bothered by a prank-playing pookie. Staff members today, as well as all through the history of the house, have described hollow footsteps along corridors when no walker is anywhere about, doors opening when nothing human is entering or leaving, and lights mysteriously turning on and off when no healthy hand is there to touch the switches.

These corny capers at Sandringham begin, for some reason, every Christmas Eve and continue for six to eight weeks. At that time Christmas cards carefully hung up so that all may see the popularity of their recipient may be moved from one wall to another at a time when the room is locked, making their owner feel just a little bit too popular—with the wrong element. Freshly made beds in rooms which have been closed and locked may be found stripped of their linen and bedding, thus causing a lot more work for someone.

One footman refused to sleep in the quarters assigned to him, because, he explained, "A large paper sack in this room breathes in and out of its own accord, like a grotesque lung." It would have done no good just to remove the sack, as one might logically suggest. Pranksters like Sandringham's would just think up something more diabolical to do.

It is the hall leading to the sergeant footman's room on the second floor, known to the servants as the Sergeant Footman's Corridor, where the haunt most frequently makes himself evident. Housemaids refuse to go there alone to clean and dust. Housemaids, 'tis said, have enough trouble with *visible* footmen sneaking up to give them a little pat or pinch. It would really be just too much if they had to put up with similar shenanigans without being able to see whom to slap.

CHAPTER THREE

Scotch–Irish Castle Hauntings

As romantic as the Irish are, and as mystical as the Scotch are, you just know that the most grisly as well as the most fascinating ghosts would be reported from their countries. Who but the Irish would have a haunt like Ormond Mallory, who rides his horse up the staircase of Castle Sheela every Christmas night—a horseman without a head?

How Ormond Mallory got to be a horseman ghost without a head is a story which begins in the famous County Limerick in 1739 when Galty Mallory, the eldest son and heir to the Castle Sheela, made the Grand Tour of the Continent. In Budapest he met and married the Countess Höja, the beautiful daughter of Count Báylor Bátoik of Illy. After a year of travel they returned to Ireland and settled down and had five children—two daughters and three sons. One of these was handsome, undisciplined, unpleasant, selfish Ormond.

Ormond inherited a fortune at the age of eighteen when his father died, and he started to live it up to the hilt immediately. His idea of a gay life was to get as many of the village maidens in trouble as he could. Or so the story

34

goes. His mother was soon so disgusted with him that she returned to Hungary with her daughters. Her parting remark to her no-good son was, "Beware of the village men. They'll surely take their revenge."

When Ormond took Moira Carmichael as his mistress, her husband John died suddenly and inexplicably. She moved into the castle but was not a good housekeeper and allowed the servants to be slack and the house to be unkempt. This didn't bother Ormond, who was the kind who had trained his horse to follow him to his bedroom. He had built a ramp alongside the staircase just for the animal, who loved him dearly. Your morals don't bother a horse, if you'll just give him a lump of sugar now and then.

In the midst of one of Moira's drunken rages, Ormond sent her packing; and he took up with a neighbor's wife. Her husband broke Ormond's shoulder. By Yuletide he was back at his old pursuits, his mother returned from Hungary, and a big party was planned for Christmas night. There was also a hunt that day, and Ormond didn't return from it when the others did. He returned much later in a very peculiar manner.

Toward midnight his horse came to the door as usual to be let in to go up to his bedroom. His russet hide was streaked and matted with dried blood. Astride his back was Ormond, tied on so he wouldn't fall off—the body of Ormond, that is, for his head was missing. It had been removed forcibly with a sharp instrument. The horse carried him up the ramp to his room and then sank to the floor, dead.

And that is why on Christmas night at Castle Sheela the

35

front door opens with a bang and the horse with its headless rider enters and clomps slowly up the stairs with its cadaverous load. Not a very pretty story, is it?

Oliver St. John Gogarty was such a competent writer that one is inclined to think perhaps a tale as beautifully written as his "The Ghost of Renvyle Castle" should be fiction. But he tells it as a factual experience in an old house he lived in which was on the westernmost tip of Ireland. His story begins when William Butler Yeats, the great Irish poet and mystic, and his young wife were honeymooning there as St. John Gogarty's guests.

"Willie," said Yeats' wife, "don't leave me to dress alone. I do not want to see that face again looking out from the glass."

This sets the stage—you know there's going to be something interesting going on that evening. Downstairs the cast was assembling. Lord Conyngham was at the ouija board, and a group gathered around him, holding a regular seance. Seymour Leslie was there, but Yeats wrote his host a note which read: "Take your friend Leslie away from us. He is a regular vortex of evil spirits." So Seymour Leslie joined Evan Morgan in the drawing room and convinced him they should hold a little seance of their own.

When St. John Gogarty and the others found Morgan later they thought he was having a fit, and until brandy revived him they almost feared for his life. "The ghost!" Morgan cried, when he came out of it. Then he told them that Seymour had locked him in the haunted room. He said he began to have a "feeling that I was all keyed up just like the tension in a nightmare, and with the terror that nightmares have. Presently, I saw a boy, stiffly upright, in brown velvet with some sort of shirt showing at his waist. He was about twelve. Behind the chair he stood, all white-faced, hardly touching the floor. It seemed that as he came nearer some awful calamity would happen to me. I was just about as tensed up as he was—nightmare terrors . . . but what made it awful was my being wide awake . . .

"But then the apparition lifted his hands to his neck, and then, all of a sudden his body was violently seized as if by invisible fiends and twisted into horrible contortions in midair. He was mad! I sympathized for a moment with his madness and felt myself at once in the electric tension of Hell. Suicide! Suicide! Oh, my God, he committed suicide in this very house!"

While they calmed Morgan, Yeats communicated with the ghost by automatic writing. The poet gave the ghost a series of commands. He must desist from frightening children in their early sleep. He must cease to moan about the chimneys. He must walk the house no more. He was ordered to name himself to Yeats and this he did—Harold Blake. He then promised to appear in the ghost room to Mrs. Yeats as he looked when he went mad sixty years before.

Mrs. Yeats, who had more foolhardy courage than I would have had, went into the room with the ghost. Presently she reappeared carrying a lighted candle. She extinguished it and moved to her husband, saying, "Yes, it is just as you said." She told him what she had seen, and he repeated it: "My wife saw a pale-faced, red-haired boy of about fourteen years of age standing in the middle of the north room. She was by the fireplace when he first took place. He had the solemn pallor of a tragedy beyond the endurance of a child. He resents the presence of strangers in the home of his ancestors. He is Harold Blake. He is to be placated with incense and flowers."

Incidentally, legend had it that the house had been built by one of the Blake family when a shipload of exotic timber was wrecked on that wild Irish coast in the eighteenth century. It's interesting how ghosts sometimes give evidence of their identity.

Sir Walter Scott spoke of the many places in Scotland which "are favorable to that degree of superstitious awe which my countrymen expressively call *eerie*." The ancient Castle of Glamis is such a place, and its secret chamber is as great a mystery today as it was over a hundred years ago, when Sir Walter was busy perpetuating the story.

The whole genius and destiny of the Scottish land makes it inevitable that its people would be aware of the unquiet spirits of the heaths and glens, and we can understand how they can still boast of their seers and wise women and their grim towers haunted by the perturbed spirits of those who caused, or suffered, evil within their walls.

The story of Macbeth, the Thane of Glamis, however doubtful in fact, is essentially true in spirit, for the beautiful Glamis Castle, dating back one thousand years in history, has been associated with royalty from its earliest days. Located at Angus in the South Highlands, where the view from the battlements is superb, Glamis was the home of Scottish kings for generations. In recent centuries it has been occupied by members of British royalty, being the ancestral home of Britain's Queen Mother. It is most

38

famous at present as being the birthplace of the reigning Queen's sister, Princess Margaret Rose. The special spooks of Glamis Castle, however, are not reputed to be any of the ancient kings or their royal consorts or offspring, but their less regal associates.

It was in the reign of James II that Alistair Lindsay, Earl of Crawford, provided the favorite legend about the occupant of the secret chamber. Alistair was a typical product of his turbulent times—one who feared neither God, man, nor the Devil. He rebelled against the king and laughed at the thunders launched toward him by the Church. His nicknames show the terror he inspired, for he was called "The Wicked Earl" and "The Tiger Earl." He was also known as "Beardie" for some reason. Perhaps he wore a beard when they were unpopular; or perhaps his beard was bigger, or redder, or in some way more outstanding. Although not a Thane of Glamis, Beardie was a frequent and privileged visitor there; and one fateful Saturday night, at Glamis Castle, he began the game of chance which was to make him a permanent resident of the place. For he insisted on prolonging his gambling into the early hours of Sunday, when the bell was about to ring for early Mass.

When his more scrupulous companions reminded him that one should not gamble on Sunday, he replied, with a shocking oath, that such things were nothing to him, and that, if he could find anyone to join him, he would go on playing till the crack of doom. The Devil likes sports like that, and naturally he put in his appearance to take Beardie up on his challenge. A clap of thunder was heard, followed by a knock on the door and the entrance of a tall dark-clad stranger. The Devil always plays for high stakes, and Alistair Lindsay, the Earl of Crawford, was no chicken, so soon they were playing for the soul of Beardie himself. Now we know what goes on in that secret chamber at Glamis Castle—Alistair Lindsay is playing an eternal game of chance with the Devil.

Another tradition ascribes the ill-name of the secret room to a dark deed of feudal times when some members of the fierce clan of Ogilvy, fleeing to Glamis for shelter from what was only too probably deserved vengeance, were shut up in the secret chamber and left to starve.

In the reign of James V, the father of Mary, Queen of Scots, a widow of the sixth Lord Glamis, whose name was Janet Douglas, was accused of conspiring to kill the King by poison and witchcraft. The King refused to save her from the extreme penalty of the law—a cruel death by burning—which the unhappy lady accordingly suffered at Edinburgh in 1537. Although Lady Glamis was much pitied by the people, who regarded her as a victim of the King's vitriolic hatred of all Douglas blood, still a typical tradition of terror grew up around her memory. It was said that, in the hidden room at Glamis, she had practiced her black art of witchcraft; and that after her dreadful death the demon who had been her familiar spirit was still imprisoned in the dark chamber, and could be heard uttering fearful cries. No matter who is responsible for them, it is those unearthly screams which echo from the supposed direction of the secret chamber which are said to be the worst of all.

Aside from these allegedly yelling and screaming occupants of the alleged secret room—the Wicked Earl, the Witch Lady, the Witch's Demon, and the starved Ogilvys—there are other famous haunts at old Glamis Castle, and these aren't nearly so apocryphal. There is a tall man in armor who is sometimes met in the corridors, and there is a pale woman's face, with great sorrowful eyes, which is seen by a startled guest at an upper window. She is undoubtedly the "Gray Lady" who is a ghost of some real substance, having been seen by several members of the royal household.

A cousin of Queen Elizabeth, the Earl of Strathmore, who now lives there, says, "There is a gray lady without a doubt. I know, because I have seen her. But only once. I happened to be wandering around the castle one night and looked into the chapel. She was there in an attitude of prayer. My reaction was one of surprise, not alarm."

Lord Strathmore's wife has never seen the gray lady, but his aunt definitely has: the Dowager Countess Granville, sister of the Queen Mother, has been quoted by the Associated Press as saying, "I have seen the ghost, but I would rather say nothing about it. One thing leads to another. My phone would never stop ringing."

Lord Strathmore told the AP that he was not planning an exorcism—as what respectable ghost fancier would? In fact, he sounded quite surprised that anyone would present such an idea to him. "Get rid of the gray lady?" he remonstrated gently. "I would not like to do that."

There is a Scottish mansion which has the sobriquet "Ike's Castle" for a very nice reason. It is historic Culzean Castle in Turnberry; and General Dwight D. Eisenhower was given a furnished apartment there for life as a token of appreciation for his leadership of the Allied Forces in World War II. It is haunted, of course, and by a beautiful girl. Isn't that sweet? Those ghouly, grisly, screaming old haunts are for the birds and banshees. Give us a story about a gorgeous gal ghost every time.

Our account of this haunting comes from Mrs. Margaret Penney, who was visiting Culzean Castle one afternoon about five o'clock when a lovely dark-haired young woman came toward her down a corridor. She wore an evening gown even at that early hour, and she said to Mrs. Penney, "It rains today."

Since the corridor was narrow, Mrs. Penney squeezed herself against the wall to let the girl go by, saying to her, "Not much room for passing when you're as plump as I am."

The young beauty answered sadly, "I do not require any room nowadays." As the girl pressed past her, Mrs. Penney says that her entire right side turned cold, and then she realized that she had been seeing a phantom and that it had actually walked straight through her side.

It was later that same month when General Eisenhower, his wife Mamie, and their two grandchildren stayed at their apartment at Culzean Castle for a while. There is no report of their having seen the ghost.

CHAPTER FOUR

Haunted American Houses

There are so many haunted houses in the United States that you wouldn't believe it, unless you started out, as I did recently, to make a tour of them. In a book titled *Prominent American Ghosts*, I have written up many of the most interesting stories I found. But there are so many other fascinating haunts that I think it would be of more value if I don't repeat myself, and so I'll deal here with some of the rest.

The house at 25 Greenough Place in Newport, Rhode Island, for instance, has real flavor. It attracts bumble bees as well as ghosts. This is because the massive three-story Fall River granite structure was erected, in 1848, by Mrs. Mary Porter, the wife of a molasses king from New Orleans. History, not legend in this case, has it that the mortar used in the building was mixed with portland cement and molasses.

The ceilings of the house are seventeen feet high. The ground floor door hinges are silver-plated, holding twelve foot doors of great weight without screws or nails. When built, this was one of the most imposing homes in the town. The Newport *Mercury* for June 7, 1856, the year it was finished, says, "We cannot point to another hall in

43

Newport quite equal to the new and beautiful house just completed for Mrs. Porter of Louisiana." The furniture corresponded to the rest of the building, the paper said, being "rich and costly without display or excess in quantity and elaborate finish, but in keeping throughout." Even so, the Porters, Southerners living in the North at a crucial period in American history, were not happy there.

This house has continued to be called a bad luck house and an unhealthy house, according to old-time Newport residents. Everyone who has lived or visited there has felt its depressing atmosphere—although perhaps I should except its present owner. Frederick Holmes, a retired Navy Captain who enjoys bridge and golf, has made the house into apartments, and each individual area may have acquired its own personal flavor. At least, those who live on the top floor penthouse are said to be perfectly happy, and to have seen no ghosts.

The best manifestation reported here, like the Borley Rectory, is a coach-and-four which rushes through the driveway after midnight. The man who has most recently reported seeing this, however, will have to be nameless. He is a prominent Newportonian, but he drinks rather excessively, and so we can't be sure which kind of glasses he was seeing the apparition through.

The most famous resident of this house was author and diplomat Richard Washburn Child, who bought it with the greatest expectations for happiness. Indeed, he waxed quite lyrical for the *News*, which gloated on Wednesday, July 17, 1929, that Ambassador Richard Washburn Child, noted author, had purchased the Porter Villa on Greenough Place. He was quoted as saying, "I chose to live permanently in Newport because it is so close to the soil upon which my forbears lived. But, in addition, I wanted my children to acquire that which I call the 'community sense.'

"This sense," he continued, "cannot be acquired today in New York, or in large upspringing cities. On this island of Newport, however, where trees grow more luxuriously than anywhere in the world, there is a community spirit and a sense of permanence of friendship which grows quite as heartily as the trees.

"There is atmosphere in the quaint old streets, where ancient and genial ghosts walk historically and reflectively—even at mid-day . . ."

Richard Washburn Child, author of *A Diplomat Looks at Europe* and numerous other books, President Harding's Ambassador to Italy, collaborator with Mussolini on his autobiography, prominent New York lawyer, died January 31, 1935. The newspapers said he died of pneumonia in a New York hospital. Funny that local Newport residents absolutely refuse to believe that. They prefer to accept the story that he fell, or jumped, over the railing on the third floor into the stair-well, and crashed to his death in the hall below. And they insist that he haunts 25 Greenough Place.

The lovely little town of Wiscasset calls itself Maine's prettiest village, and it has good reason to. It also, if some local residents are to be believed, could be known as Maine's most haunted town. The Smith House on High Street is famous for its ghost, a little old lady who sits and rocks by the window; but I found several others as well. In fact, right next door to the Smith House is the Musical Wonder House, which may also be haunted. Robert

Miller, who works there as a guide and receptionist, thinks so, and he should know because he sees the ghost there.

The owners of the house, Danilo Konvalinka and Douglas Henderson, are more willing to attribute reports of this nature to the activity of squirrels or bats in the attic. I agreed with them that squirrels and bats in attics do account for many ghosts, and squirrely people with bats in their belfries account for most of the rest. Yet there are always a few cases which have responsible enough witnesses testifying to their authenticity to keep us wondering, and to warrant investigation. And perhaps their house is one of these.

Even these skeptical men admit, however, that doors here do close by themselves when there is no draft and that various people have reported hearing noises, not only from the attic but from other rooms, which made them think that children were talking and playing somewhere. They didn't sound to anybody like squirrels or bats—they sounded like children. This house has twenty-three rooms and fifteen working fireplaces, and it would be difficult to track down such noises in time to explain them. But this one fact was known: No youngsters were in the house at the time when such childish chatter occurred.

The reason the house is so large, incidentally, is that it was originally built as a duplex back in 1852, but then one owner bought out the other and had the walls between removed. He then installed one of the most perfect examples of a flying staircase in the country. (A flying staircase just starts at the bottom and goes straight up to the top. It has no supports of any kind.)

Even with the other manifestations in the house which are unaccountable, Robert Miller is kidded when he claims to see the ghost. But he maintains his right to freedom of speech and says he knows what he sees and nobody is going to talk him out of it. It was sometime during the winter of 1965–1966 that he first saw his own private apparition in the Musical Wonder House, which, I should explain, is a museum for mechanical music boxes of all kinds. He was on the couch in the sitting room. As he glanced around he thought he saw something peering at him through the doorway, and then it seemed to go upstairs. Robert says, "I looked around thinking it might be a cat, although it didn't look like a cat. But anyway, there was no cat in the house, nor anybody else. I searched carefully."

The next time he saw it he was in the kitchen in the early spring of 1966. "I was at the stove working with my back to the sink," he says. "As I turned around I saw out of the corner of my eye a young man in his late teens or early twenties. It was a gray outline, like a cloud of mist going by the door. I thought it was a person, yet I didn't know what it was, because it darted so quick." Miller continues to have a feeling that he is being watched, and occasionally since then he has thought he saw his gray ghost going by doorways. He doesn't guarantee anything, but he is quite sure that he is not a person deluded by his own imagination.

There's another ghost in Wiscasset, too. I am inclined to think that the people there cherish their haunts—the operator of the quaint Eastwind Restaurant certainly does. Dorothy F. Apgar says she has a poltergeist-like haunt which came with her house and which will probably remain there if she has anything to do with it. She tolerates it graciously, even though it is rough on her personally.

The restaurant is in an old house built in 1800 on the

main street of the town. It contained Wiscasset's earliest apothecary shop, and it was here, I was told, that the first ice cream in America was made, and served to General Lafayette when he visited there. The builder of the house was Charles Dana; and his wife, or some other relative, was Lydia, known as Mother Dana. It is she who is said to have remained with the structure through its various metamorphoses from apothecary shop to tea room.

For some reason, Lydia only manifests in the daytime, but she does it in various ways, from making a latched door open by itself to tipping trays and spilling food when waitresses are going through the hall door. On one Mother's Day two teapots on the same table where a special party was being held were turned upside down. (Wouldn't Nandor Fodor have had fun with the psychological implications of this spook?)

At the Eastwind Restaurant, I learned, chairs move by themselves, too. Not only Dorothy Apgar has seen these various manifestations, but others of her employees as well—although I had to take her word for that. The only helper of hers with whom I was able to talk was a former employee who had definitely, he claimed, seen the latched door open by itself. He was—you guessed it—the ubiquitous Robert Miller who now works at the Musical Wonder House.

Lydia's main malevolence is directed at Dorothy Apgar. Only recently she gave her a big wallop on the back while she was standing before the window in the front room. Often she treats her rougher than that, keeping her ensconced in plaster much of the time.

"I'm always being pushed downstairs," says Mrs. Apgar. "For three years in a row I have been in a cast—broken knee . . . broken foot . . . it's gotten so that when friends leave in the fall they say, 'Now, Dorothy, don't break anything this winter!' " Her latest experience of this kind was during the winter of 1966 when she stood on a small footstool about one foot high. It was one hundred and fifty years old but solid, she insists. Yet with her on it, it suddenly collapsed. Result—the broken foot.

With such unpleasantness going on in her house, wouldn't you think Dorothy would wish to have Lydia forcibly removed? "No," she says defiantly, "I'm going to keep her. I'll win her over with love."

There's a delightful old ghost in New York State in what is known as the Mohawk Valley, where, among peaceful farms one suddenly comes upon a real Scottish castle. The ghost built it, and she loved it, and she wouldn't leave it for anything, so she now haunts it, cantankerously insisting that everything remain as it was when she lived there. The ghost is known as "Aunt Harriet" because a niece inherited the castle from her.

When she was in her earthly abode she was known as Harriet Douglas Cruger, a red-haired, wilful, independent woman—who was also a most extraordinary human being. She was born in 1790 and her parents died when she was quite young, leaving her with 16,000 acres of wilderness in the Mohawk Valley, a house in New York City, and a considerable fortune. She was not satisfied, as she grew up, to be merely one of the belles of New York. She had to conquer Europe as well. Every year from 1821 to 1833 she went abroad, with all her servants and a vast amount of luggage. She was definitely no beauty, but she must have had a certain charm, because she surely managed to meet almost everyone famous of her day. A word picture of her painted by Sir Walter Scott is far from flattering, however. In his diary for July 1, 1828, he wrote:

"Miss Douglas dined with us, a professed lion huntress, who travels the country to raise the peaceful beasts out of their lair, and insists on being hand and glove with all the leonine races. She is very plain, besides frightfully red-haired . . . an awful visitation! I think I see her with javelin raised and buckskin foot, a second Diana, roaming the hills of Westmoreland in quest of the Lakers. Would to God she were there, or anywhere but here! Affectation is painful to witness, and this poor woman has the bad taste to think direct flattery is the way to make advances to friendship and intimacy."

Just how intimate she became with Scott, despite his protests, we have no way of knowing; but on the mantle of her castle today is a green glass drinking cup embossed with silver thistles, a souvenir from him.

The portrait of her hanging in her castle shows the Scottish author to have been quite accurate in his description. She's not only plain, but she has a cross look on her face. She has a dumpy figure, and she is certainly frightfully red-haired. Nonetheless, she's bedecked in silver lace and green velvet and sitting as proudly as any great beauty might in the costume she wore when presented to King William IV.

The haughty Harriett found the love of her life when she visited her uncle and aunt in their Scottish Castle Gelsten. She determined to have a home as nearly like it as possible, and indeed it was from her drawings and plans of Gelsten that her own castle in New York State was built. She furnished Henderson House, as her castle is called, with rugs and mahoganies, linen, glass, silver, and damasks that she brought back with her from every yearly foray abroad.

How can a woman build a whole castle by herself? She didn't. By that time, when she was over forty, she had finally decided to get married. Or perhaps, considering her looks, it was only then that she had found a man willing to marry her. Anyway, in 1833 she was wed to Henry Cruger, a lawyer from New York City. They lived together, when their Scottish castle in the American wilderness was finally finished, for the rest of their lives, although it was probably a pretty hectic existence, owing to Harriett's hot temper. She laid down all the laws around the place; she was forever slamming doors when in a rage; and once, when peeved at her husband, she had their double bed sawed in half.

Harriett had definitely created a little bit of Scotland in the United States. She even brought all her servants from the old country, with their customs unchanged. She had them play their bagpipes and dance their Highland Flings, and the family was always summoned to dinner by the notes of "Up with the Bonnets of Bonny Dundee."

When she died at the age of eighty in 1870, Harriett left orders that she was to be buried in a stone sarcophagus in the basement of the castle. Instead, her heirs put her in the cemetery and used the sarcophagus for a horse trough. Soon they got their first hint that death had not cooled Aunt Harriett's hot temper: the stone horse trough was smashed by lightning. From then on whenever anything around the house is not done the way Harriett used to prefer it, she lets them know in no uncertain terms that she is dissatisfied. Doors slam just as vehemently as they did when she was alive, bells ring, teacups are snatched out of the maids' hands and smashed to bits on the floor. (But never teacups which belonged to Aunt Harriett.) Objects are removed from tables, pictures swing on walls. And the great organ which Harriett had installed, and with which she used to rouse guests at dawn, groans even when no human hands are on the keyboard. Aunt Harriett is still running her magic Scottish castle, and no one need forget it.

In the State of Virginia, a stately and serene mansion named Westover on the James River is the home of one of America's most attractive ghosts. Over the years the wraith of Evelyn Byrd has appeared often, and she has been so solidly corporeal that those who saw her have always mistaken her at first for a living woman.

This house, a landmark of pre-Revolutionary Virginia, was the home of William Byrd and his lovely daughter, whom he took to England in 1717 to be educated and presented at court. There she fell hopelessly in love with a nobleman who is said to have been Charles Mordaunt, the grandson of the Earl of Peterborough. Because Mordaunt was a Catholic, William Byrd refused to allow his daughter to marry him; and he abruptly brought Evelyn back home to Westover. There she languished, rejecting all other suitors, living as a lonely exile. And there she declined and died of a broken heart at the age of twenty-nine.

Before she died, Evelyn told a friend that if she could she would return to see Westover. Why she would want to come back to an earth which had given her such a bad time, is hard to understand. But apparently she has done so, as the families who have lived in Westover since then all adamantly maintain.

A halcyon in Greek mythology was a bird which, floating on the sea in its nest, hatched its young at the time of the winter solstice, magically having a peaceful, calming influence on the waters. Thus, when the nation's first Secretary of the Navy, Benjamin Stoddert, named the home he built in 1783 "Halcyon House" he expected it to be a place of peace, calmness, and quiet. What he produced, instead, was a haunted house. Located at 3400 Prospect Street, in Georgetown, a suburb of Washington, D.C., the house is still the beautiful mansion it always was, even though it has now been sold to Georgetown University, which plans to turn it into a woman's dormitory. It faces the Potomac River, with a magnificent garden running down to the river from the front door, which has a seven-section fanlight flanked by fluted pilasters with a rounded arch and keystone above it.

At the turn of the century an eccentric named Albert Clemens owned the house, and he refused to allow electricity—that new-fangled foolishness—to be installed. He did install, however, a large cigar store Indian on the balcony overlooking the front door. Clemens is said to have been buried under a chapel in the house.

Before its recent sale the place was owned by George S. Roper, whose son Nick has expressed himself freely about the ghost to the newspapers. He told about footsteps that tread the attic and run up and down the stairs, lights that switch on and off without human hands, doors that open and shut themselves, and ashtrays that mysteriously fill with water, of all things.

Nick Roper said: "My twenty-one-year-old sister Anne and the three girls who share Apartment 1214 will admit they have heard strange things, too. The girls report that every Thursday between one and two in the morning they hear measured pacing in the attic overhead. The ghost is always on schedule."

Roper continued: "On two or three occasions my mother Mary, while brewing coffee in the kitchen, heard someone running down the stairs. Convinced it was me, she poured a cup and waited. When I didn't show up, she came upstairs calling me. I was still in my room and hadn't left it.

"Night after night, I have heard footsteps in the attic over my room, sometimes on the fire escape outside my French window. They pace steadily, then stop abruptly. The first time this happened, thinking it might be a prowler, I sneaked up into the attic to check. The light was on, but no one was there. The only way out of the attic was through my bedroom. I shrugged off the burning light as an electrical quirk (although the switch worked perfectly) and the footsteps as the normal creakings of an old house." This is quite natural, of course. We must be alert not to be taken in by the creakings of old houses, birds in chimneys, squirrels in attics, or bats in belfries.

But one time Nick Roper found the lights burning in the basement and the atmosphere surcharged with the presence of an Unseen Person. When he shouted, "Who's there?" the light went out by itself. On another occasion he was awakened to find himself floating above his bed. He was gently lowered to his couch again by unseen hands. Nick was probably just as well pleased when his family moved out of that house.

There is a theory that Secretary Stoddert is the ghost that haunts this place. But certainly a man who would name his home Halcyon House would never be the one to cause it the unpleasantness of a haunting. I prefer to blame it all on Albert Clemens and his cigar store Indian.

If you should decide to hunt in North Carolina for the House in the Horseshoe, take a good road map with you or you may have a few problems. Located in a large curving bend of the Deep River in northern Moore County, the house had an interesting, if small, role in the American Revolution, at least enough to get itself shot full of bullet holes. It is also haunted.

Usually known as the Alston House because Colonel Philip Alston was an early owner, the House in the Horseshoe was built about 1770—one of the first "big houses" in the frontier country of upland North Carolina. On Sunday, August 5, 1781, Col. Alston, leader of a band of North Carolina Whig fighters, was camped with his men at his home. Early in the morning, David Fanning, a notorious Tory commander, with his larger force of men, attacked the Whigs barricaded in the building. After a brisk two-hour battle, during which numerous bullet holes were inflicted on the house itself, the Tories attempted to set the place on fire by rolling a cartload of burning straw against it. Surrendering seemed to be the better part of valor at this point, and so a white flag was carried out of the house by Col. Alston's wife.

This kind of informal hit-and-run fighting between Whig and Tory bands was frequent during the Revolution in that part of the country, and Alston and his men were soon released on parole. Alston, though a prominent and influential member of an excellent family, was a turbulent person and was frequently in trouble with the law. Finally, after being implicated in what the Moore County Historical Association pamphlet calls "a probable murder," he left the state. He died the next year, and being such a trouble-prone character, maybe he is the ghost.

One could hardly suspect as the culprit the next owner, a gentleman of the dignity of Benjamin Williams, who was Governor of North Carolina for four terms. Williams had been a brave officer in the Revolution, had served in Congress, and had been a member of the first board of trustees of the University of North Carolina. He built up the 3,000 acres in the Horseshoe into one of the state's first large cotton plantations. In 1803 he valued his plantation at $30,000 and he had between fifty and sixty slaves.

Following Williams' death there in 1814, the land changed ownership many times. By 1954 the house had reached such a state of deterioration that the Moore County Historical Association rescued it and restored it. It is the present caretaker, E. M. Landreth, and his wife Flossie, who gave my best testimony about the ghost; although the place has a history throughout the state as a haunted house.

It seems that the first evidence of haunting within recent memory occurred at the time of the death of a former owner, Anderson Jones, he of the long beard whose picture hangs over the upstairs mantle. George Hardin, who lived on the property, and another man were sitting up beside his deathbed in one of the downstairs rooms. Suddenly they heard a sound reverberate from one corner of the house to the other—as if fingers were striking across a guitar. The other man said quickly, "I got to get a drink of water," and he went outside to the well. When he didn't come back after a reasonable length of time, George Hardin followed him, and found him "taking off" down the road. George ran and caught up with him and made him come back, although the man was reluctant because the slithering fingers on the guitar strings had frightened him so. Just as they returned to the house Jones died.

Landreth recalls hearing many tales about the place. It was said that there used to be some kind of a light that came out of the ground on the plantation and would go up into the air. But nothing like that ever happened during the nine years he and his wife and their ten children lived in the house. Landreth is very careful to relate only his own personal experiences, or those of members of his family—and they were enough. They frequently, for instance, would hear doors which were definitely shut sound as if they were being dragged open and shut, and somebody walking up and down the steps when nobody was there. "It got so there was something like this about every night," Landreth said. Members of the family weren't scared particularly, and would get up and hunt to see what it was; but they never could find the source of their puzzlement.

At one time when son James Ronald was about eighteen or nineteen he was sleeping regularly in the front room downstairs. He frequently heard someone whispering in the fireplace. He could hear it plainly, but could never make out what was said. When I asked Mr. Landreth if James Ronald was positive he was not hearing birds in the chimney, I was assured that his son would know the difference between the sound of birds in the chimney and people whispering. But in a haunted house, when you are expecting every little commotion to be a spooky one, I wonder who can really be sure.

Both Mr. and Mrs. Landreth independently told me

their favorite story—about their daughters who were in the house one day when they heard footsteps go up the stairs and then go down again. Since no one else was home except Mrs. Landreth and they were sure she had gone out, Mr. Landreth says, "to get some taters," they were surprised. "I thought mamma said she was going up to the barn," said one of the girls, and the other replied, "She did, and yonder she comes now." They rushed to ask her if she had just come back and gone upstairs, but she had not. No one else had either.

Mrs. Landreth said that one night she heard the hall door drag open. Then from the corner of her bed she heard a "zizzing like a bee. It was as if the bedsprings were zizzing." But when she got up close to that corner of the bed, the racket didn't come from there after all. It then sounded as if it were out in the hall. But when she went into the hall the vibration seemed to come from her room. She went back and forth in an attempt to learn what was going on. "I did that," she said, "I bet you a solid hour, but I never did find out what was causing it."

The Carolinas are famous for fabulous old homes with fabulous old phantoms, but as a friend and I drove down the coast of South Carolina heading for Charleston, we didn't have our minds on ghosts at all. As we rode along, my friend said, "Wouldn't it be nice to stop at some old plantation just to see it?" I agreed, and so we looked for signs inviting visitors to some of the showplaces. When we were about forty miles north of Charleston my eye caught a roadside poster saying "Hampton" and pointing off to the right. Although this was coincidence, the details of what happened after that seem to me to be almost more than coincidence. In fact, I think the Hampton ghost somehow connived to get us there so that it would be included in this book. Well, sometimes I do.

At the bottom of the Hampton sign was the statement that we should inquire at a filling station, and there was one across the road; but when I mentioned it to my friend she thought it must mean some other station nearer to the house. So we turned onto the side road leading toward Hampton and proceeded boldly forward. If we had stopped at the designated filling station, of course, we would have learned that the house was closed to visitors. Instead, we drove about a mile down a country lane, and then came to a sign saying "Hampton." It also said "Closed." It added that this was the home of Archibald Rutledge.

I shrieked, "Oh, this house is haunted!" I had read that Mr. Rutledge, the Poet Laureate of South Carolina, had a family ghost at his plantation. So even though we were supposed to keep out, when we'd come that far toward a ghost house we felt compelled to try at least to see the outside of it. The road was blocked by a heavy chain, so we left the car here.

It was a simmeringly hot September noon as we walked down the dusty lane toward Hampton, and mosquitoes treated us in a most unfriendly fashion. But we plugged persistently onward for about half a mile. Then we found our way barred by a large gate, which was fastened together in the middle by a heavy chain and lock. The wire fence on each side of it had a barbed top. It all looked forbidding enough to have balked any explorers less determined than we. Debating about whether we might find some spot whereby we could crawl under the fence, and rather hoping not to, because the bushy terrain around there could easily have been snakey, we decided that a forcible attack in the area of the gate was our only hope of successful entry.

"Let me try to lift this side," I said, "and perhaps we can get under it." However, when I applied a little leverage I discovered that the gate was much too heavy for me to move. But, as I said, this house wanted us to visit it. So just then the rusty old hinges came loose from the post and the entire left half of the gate just lay over on its side. We stepped in, deciding—whether the law would agree with us or not—that we couldn't be considered trespassers when the gate had laid itself down and invited us to walk over it.

There was still a good brisk hike to reach the house, although we were neither brisk nor hiking by then. What we were doing was wilting along, swatting mosquitoes. I only hope when George Washington was at Hampton for breakfast (as I later read in a Charleston library) that the insects were better behaved.

When the house finally hove into view, it was worth all our struggle to get to it. Lurking amidst magnificent live oak trees decorated with gray Spanish moss, it looked lost and forsaken; but it well remembered its past days of grandeur, and its massive loveliness was evident even though it needed a paint job. Actually, it was a much better haunted house the way it was; but refurbished, as it would be before the tourist season began, Hampton would be able to hold its own with any stately mansion in the country.

We wandered about and took pictures and fought mosquitoes and climbed up on the huge veranda and admired its eight great pillars. As we looked we called out to any ghosts who might be around the deserted place, begging them to make an appearance for us, to look out the windows, to scream, to do something. But the house merely stared back at us with the blank look an uninhabited house always wears. No specter showed itself and nothing spoke to us.

The haunt of this house is really not much of a character anyway. Its only claim to reality that I know of comes from Rutledge's brief mention of it in *My Colonel and His Lady* (The Bobbs-Merrill Co., Inc., Indianapolis, 1937), where he says:

"Like all other self-respecting plantation houses, Hampton had a ghost. This creature made its presence known from time to time by a remarkably regular series of sounds. First there would be a soft monotonous noise as if some grandmother were quietly rocking in a chair. And these sounds always were heard coming from my great-grandmother's bedroom, immediately over the dining room. Then there would be three distinct raps, after which would come a creepy sound as if someone were guiltily and surreptitiously dragging a heavy body across the room overhead, always from the northwest to the southeast corner. Three more raps would conclude the weird performance. I can remember that, not infrequently, as we were at tea, or while we were reading in the dining room afterward, this weird rite would be gone through, and one of us would say casually, so familiar did it become, 'There's the ghost.'

"With lanterns and pokers and even with guns, also with a trepidation that diminished each time we went, we visited the room whence the sounds had come, but never did we come to any possible sort of an explanation—unless a rat made the curious series of identical sounds."

But if the ghost in this house was slightly routine, the

history of discovered buried treasure is fascinating. The property on which the mansion is built has been in the possession of Archibald Rutledge's ancestors since 1686. The house was built about 1735 by Nöe Serré, a grandson and namesake of one of the Huguenot emigrants who settled this part of the country. Archibald Rutledge was born at Hampton and lived there until he was about twelve. In August, 1937, when he was fifty-six, he returned to the house to live after an absence of forty-four years. He now spends part of the year there and part in Spartanburg.

When he first returned to Hampton, Rutledge explored the house thoroughly. While he didn't find the ghost, he did find a secret room and a map—and how many haunted houses have ever before given up their secret treasure?

In *Home by the River*, he said that there is a high passageway between the living room and the ballroom. On the left of the passageway is a secret closet, concealed by wallpaper that covers the wall and the door. On the right of this high passageway is a similar offset, but this runs clear to the roof and had never been opened. There had always been a strong family tradition that this room might contain something—treasure, perhaps, or a skeleton! So one day Rutledge and his helper, Lewis, went into the ballroom cellar and sawed through the floor into the mysterious compartment.

When the sheer blackness of the compartment was apparent, Lewis' courage failed him, and he was *hors de combat* for the rest of the day. But Rutledge "climbed up into it with a flashlight. All was dust and darkness and silence." He found a small box, however, but the lightness of it was disappointing. Inside the box was a folded paper on which he discovered a plan of the house. "From one corner, a line was drawn at a certain angle, 34 feet 11½ inches. There was even a drawing of a shovel so that the finder of the map would know what to do." Also on the map was a cross and a picture of a box that looked like a treasure chest. "But on that exact spot grows a live oak a century old. I have not yet delved for this treasure. But I must. I believe I shall find it."

Rutledge says he has already discovered some of the buried treasure, however. As he was putting up a work-bench in one of the cellars, he noticed that the floor consisted of more than a foot of solid ashes and sand. Stirring through this mixture, he found an assortment of relics: bushels of broken Wedgewood china, old brass locks and homemade fasteners, numerous hinges, and ancient bottles. To add to this antique collector's dream come true, he discovered hand-blown glass, brass escutch-eons, antique razors, spectacles, and implements for hand-loading shotgun shells.

His best find to date of this nature was made in one of the west cellars. Under a two-foot thick layer of ashes were twenty-eight Delft tiles, some of which must already have been antiques when they were brought over to America, hundreds of years ago. Some of these tiles are even signed by the artists who made them.

Rutledge wasn't satisfied. He continued poking around for the treasure indicated on the map. One morning, as he was probing in the sand-and-leaf mould near the live oak, he struck something at a depth of about four feet and unearthed a small stone crock which had been sealed fast.

Hurrying into the house, he pried open the crock, amazed that so small an article should seem so heavy. At first, his reaction was one of bitter disappointment. The contents of the crock seemed to be nothing more than a stained old newspaper, a copy of the Charleston *Mercury* dated early in April, 1861, which contained an account of the battle of Fort Sumter, the opening battle of the Civil War.

Then came the actual treasure. Wrapped in long strips of the newspaper were 198 American gold coins. Rutledge quickly put two and two together and decided that his grandfather hid the coins, fearing the possibility of looting and plundering during the war.

A bit of study convinced Rutledge how tremendously valuable the coins truly were. "The dates began with the very beginning of our gold coinage in 1795 and ended with 1861.

". . . many of the coins had been privately minted . . . a ten-dollar gold piece of 1849 [was] stamped Kellogg and Co., California, another was stamped Deseret, Utah and had . . . been minted by the Mormons. There were other privately minted coins . . ." adding to a tremendous value, not only in cash but as a real find for the serious coin collector.

All of these coins seemed to be of pure gold—bright yellow and very beautiful. The Government allowed Rutledge to keep them because they had been family heirlooms, and so he decided to divide them between his three sons when they returned from serving in World War II. One of his sons did not return, but the treasure has been given to the other two.

New Orleans, Louisiana, one of the most glamorous cities in the United States, has countless ghosts to its credit. One of its most interesting haunted houses is on Chartres Street in the old French Quarter—the Vieux Carré—directly opposite the ancient Convent of the Ursulines. The house now belongs to the famous author Frances Parkinson Keyes, but it is not hers alone. General Beauregard, the Civil War hero, continues to share the home he used to live in, and, if tradition is true, he refights the Battle of Shiloh every night.

Built in 1812 by Joseph leCarpentier, this old mansion is frequently referred to as the most beautiful house in the Vieux Carré. Granite staircases decorated with the wrought-iron lacework so typical of old New Orleans, curve gracefully from each end of its high front gallery; and tall iron gates stand like twin sentinels on guard in front of the house.

When Pierre Gustave Toutant-Beauregard moved there he was a young Major, fresh from the Mexican war. He lived in the house, except for the years he was away from it fighting in the Civil War, until 1869. And he lives in it still. If you don't believe me, listen to those who have spent a night in the house—alone, with the candles unlit and the doors barred. About two A.M., they say, all the exquisite period furniture in the magnificent front hall and the surrounding rooms fades away. Then the huge doors of the ballroom open and out comes the General in his shabby, faded gray uniform. As he walks, men spring up from every side—the ragged remnants of a great struggle. And all around them is the battlefield of Shiloh. Night after night the hell of war is revived here.

Maybe this is just a folktale. Yet again, maybe it is smoke from a very real fire. Remember what I said in the Introduction about memory images?

65

CHAPTER FIVE

Ghosts in Canadian Houses

One of the most prominent ghosts ever to appear in Canada was a famous poet from the United States—Walt Whitman. He happened to make his apparitional visit there because a very close friend of his was dying in Bon Echo, Ontario, on Mazinaw Lake. At Bon Echo is a majestic bluff some two miles in length and three or four hundred feet high, which is known as Bon Echo Rock. On it are Algonquin paintings and in it, according to legend, is a lost Indian treasure cave. On a point on the crest of this bluff there is a crag which sometimes seems to look like a bewhiskered man. This has been dedicated as a memorial to the American poet and is known familiarly as "Old Walt."

It was for the 1919 dedication ceremony of this memorial that Horace Traubel came to Bon Echo. Traubel, a warm personal friend of the poet's, has been called his Boswell, because he wrote several volumes about him. He was also one of the literary executors of Whitman's estate. While he was staying at the home of Mrs. Flora MacDonald Denison, it became evident that Traubel's heart ailment, from which he had previously been suffering, was becoming increasingly worse. He spent his last days at

Mrs. Denison's home, and during that time she noted several rather unusual things which impressed her so much that she made notes of them at the time and later wrote of them. They were published in 1920 in a little magazine called *The Sunset of Bon Echo;* and later at the request of the Society for Psychical Research Mrs. Denison secured the signed statement of the man who had shared with Mr. Traubel the experience of seeing the ghost of Walt Whitman.

On the evening of August 28, 1919, Mr. Traubel sat for a while on the veranda with his wife, looking over at the great rock called "Old Walt." Later as he was being carried in, his face became radiant. "Look! look! Flora," he cried, "quick! quick! he's going!"

"What, where, Horace?" Mrs. Denison answered. "I don't see anyone."

"Why, just over the rock Walt appeared, head and shoulders and with his hat on—in a golden glory—brilliant and splendid. He reassured me, beckoned to me, and spoke to me. I heard his voice, but didn't understand all he said, only, 'Come on.'"

His vision cheered Traubel immensely, and he told several of his visitors about it. The change in his morale was remarkable, but the watchers at his bedside realized that his physical strength was failing rapidly. On the night of September 3rd he was very low. As Mrs. Denison was turning him over at his request, he suddenly seemed to be listening.

"I hear Walt's voice," he said. "He's talking to me."

"What does he say?" Mrs. Denison asked.

"Walt says, 'Come on, come on.'" Then he added, "Flora, I see them all about me, Bob and Bucke and Walt and the rest." He was referring to two other of their mutual friends who had preceded him in death, Robert Ingersoll and Richard M. Bucke, the author of *Cosmic Consciousness*. We could, of course, think of this as the seeing of typical deathbed apparitions, were it not for the experience of Mr. Cosgrave.

Whether or not it was significant, it seemed so to Mrs. Denison and Mrs. Traubel when one night shortly thereafter they were on the veranda and saw a huge eagle circling round and round. Mrs. Denison referred to Ingersoll's statement about Walt Whitman as "an eagle soaring above the theological chickadees and sparrows." Just then the eagle screamed and flew away into the bright moonlight.

The person who actually shared Traubel's experience of seeing Whitman's ghost, Colonel L. Moore Cosgrave, came in to sit up with the patient during his last three nights on earth. He said in the report he later wrote on the apparition for the American Society for Psychical Research that Traubel, while unable to move, seemed to be perfectly conscious, and evidently in no pain. His eyes gave the suggestion of his needs. In the early morning hours, about 3 o'clock, he grew perceptibly weaker. Cosgrave wrote, "A little later his lips moved as if he were trying to speak. I put back his head, thinking he needed more air, but he moved again and his eyes remained riveted on a spot some three feet above the bed. At last my own eyes were irresistibly drawn to the same point in the darkness—there was but a small, shaded light behind the curtain on the farther side of the room.

"Slowly, the point at which we were both looking grew gradually brighter, and then a light haze appeared. It

68

spread until it assumed bodily form, and it had the likeness to Walt Whitman, standing beside the bed, a rough tweed jacket on, an old felt hat on his head and his right hand in his pocket. He was gazing down at Traubel, a kindly reassuring smile on his face. He nodded twice as though reassuringly. The features were quite distinct for at least a full minute, then the figure gradually faded from sight."

While both the dying man and his friend were gazing at the apparition it moved closer to Traubel. "There's Walt," he murmured. At that instant the apparition passed through the bed to Colonel Cosgrave and touched his hand. "I distinctly felt it as though I had touched an electric charge," he says. "He then smiled at his dying friend and passed from our sight." Two days later Traubel died.

The first mayor of Toronto, who was also the grandfather of Prime Minister William Lyon Mackenzie King, is Canada's most famous ghost. He and some of his female relatives manage to keep spectacularly busy haunting their old home at 82 Bond Street in Toronto, which has been preserved as a national shrine. These haunts may have been part of the reason that the late Prime Minister Mackenzie King, who helped make Canada great and prosperous during his twenty-two years in office, was himself a confirmed believer in the ability of spirits of the dead to communicate with the living. For political reasons he did not allow his interest in this to be publicized during his life. His exploration of the supernormal remained his strictly private affair until after his death in 1950; but then it was reported in several publications.

The Prime Minister's grandfather, William Lyon

Mackenzie was born in Dundee, Scotland, in 1795 and later emigrated to Canada. He founded a newspaper called *The Colonial Advocate* and in it he rebelled against the government with such fiery attacks that he became a hero to the people. He was elected to the Legislative Assembly of Upper Canada and reelected five times. Then he was chosen Toronto's first mayor. But it is since his death in his house on Bond Street in 1861 that he's been the biggest rebel—against the conformity of resting peacefully in his grave, or so we are led to believe by the accounts of the families who have tried to live there. For a while after Mackenzie's death one of his daughters had a girls' school in the house. It is now run as a museum of early Canadiana by the William Lyon Mackenzie Homestead Foundation.

It is to an article by Andrew MacFarlane in The Toronto *Telegram* that we are indebted for a complete account of the problems the Foundation has keeping a resident caretaker in the building. There is a nice apartment on the top floor where the caretakers and their families might live, but its rooms are frequently vacant because the haunt scares away anyone who attempts to live there. Let's listen to the report of Mr. and Mrs. Alex Dobban, who moved into the third floor apartment in April, 1960. They planned to look after the house for a small salary to supplement Mr. Dobban's pension and have a rent-free apartment. It seemed like a wonderful arrangement for them; but they only stayed there a month.

Mr. Dobban told The Toronto *Telegram*, "We couldn't stay any longer because of the effect the place was having on my wife's nerves. The things she heard were getting her down . . . she couldn't stand to stay overnight."

Mrs. Dobban said, "We hadn't been here long when I heard footsteps going up the stairs. I called to my husband, but he wasn't there. There was no one else in the house. But I heard feet on the stairs." One night Mrs. Dobban woke up and heard the press going in the basement. This is a printing press purchased by Mackenzie in 1825 which is still in working order, but is kept locked up. That doesn't bother the ghost, who probably has the key.

Mrs. Dobban also heard the piano playing when she and her husband were in bed and no one else was in the house. It is a little old-fashioned upright which stands in the front parlor downstairs. Mr. Dobban heard none of the sounds his wife did; but she insisted that while she did not believe in ghosts, she knew of no other explanation. At the time she heard these sounds, she did not know what had happened to the people who had lived there before them.

Mr. and Mrs. Charles Edmunds had managed to hold out there for three years, but they had finally left just before the Dobbans came. Mrs. Edmunds had lost almost forty pounds because of the mounting tension she was under during those three years. She heard the footsteps, right from the first, and fortunately her husband also heard them, so they could compare notes. Mrs. Edmunds told the *Telegram* reporter: "One night I woke up at midnight to see a lady standing over my bed . . . leaning over me. There's no room for anyone to stand where she was because the bed is pushed up against the wall. She was hanging down, like a shadow, but I could see her clearly. Something seemed to touch me on the shoulder to wake me up. She had long hair hanging down in front of her shoulders, dark brown, I think. She had a long narrow face. Then she was gone.

"Two years ago, early in March, I saw the lady again. It was the same—except this time she reached out and hit me. When I woke up my left eye was purple and blood-shot.

"I also saw the man at night, a little bald man in a frock coat. I would just see him for a few seconds and then he would vanish."

Mr. Edmunds thinks it is evidential that all the pictures in the homestead show Mackenzie with hair on his head, yet the man his wife saw and described to him was completely bald with side whiskers. She had not read anything about the old gentleman, but Mr. Edmunds had. So he knew, when she didn't, that Mackenzie was actually bald and wore a wig.

Mrs. Edmunds says:

"My son and his wife heard the piano playing at night when they were staying with us. When my husband and my son went to look—it stopped.

"We could feel the homestead shaking with a rumbling noise some nights. It must have been the press in the basement. We thought at first it might be the subway. But we were too far from the subway . . .

"I did not believe in ghosts when I went to stay at the Mackenzie Homestead. But I do now. It's the only expla-nation I can think of. I wish to say that I would not say anything against the Mackenzies. They were hard-working people and so are we. They were not hard on us. It's just that the house was a strain on the nerves."

Mr. Edmunds still doesn't believe in the supernatural, but he doesn't know what else it was—there certainly was "something peculiar about the place." On one occasion, just after they had moved in, he said, "my two grandchildren, Susan (then age four) and Ronnie (then age three) went from the upstairs bedroom down to the second floor bathroom at night. A few minutes later there were terrific screams. I went down and they were both huddled in the bathroom, terrified. They said there was a lady in the bathroom. I asked where she was now and they said she just disappeared.

"On another occasion something peculiar happened with some flowers we had in pots on a window ledge inside the house. This was in winter and we had the geraniums inside. We watered the plants twice a week, on Sundays and Wednesdays. On a Saturday morning we found that they all had been watered, although we hadn't done it. There was water spilled all over the plants and the saucers they were standing in were full. There was mud on the curtains and holes in the earth as if someone had poked their fingers in. There was water on the dressing table. Neither of us had watered the plants and neither had anyone else.

"We often heard footsteps on the stairs. Thumping footsteps like someone with heavy boots. This happened frequently when there was no one in the house but us, when we were sitting together upstairs.

"The whole house used to shake with a rumbling sound sometimes. My wife is convinced that this was Mackenzie's press.

"I am not an imaginative man and I do not believe in ghosts. But the fact is that the house was strange enough so that we had to leave."

The Toronto paper also got statements from the Edmunds' son, Robert, and his wife, Minnie, who had stayed with them when they first moved into Mackenzie

House. Robert said that his wife woke him one night, saying that she heard the piano playing downstairs. "I heard it too," he said. "I cannot remember what the music was like, but it was the piano downstairs playing." They both heard the music three or four different times, and they heard the printing press run once.

The newspaper reporter himself spent a night in the haunted house with photographer Joe Black. As is so often the case when investigators are on the alert for ghostly phenomena, absolutely nothing occurred. Let me hasten to state that this does not prove for one minute that the witnesses had been fabricating their stories or that they were hysterical and had dreamed them up. It only means that conditions have to be right for things like this to happen. If the people living in a house were to try to set a trap for their ghosts, they probably would have no results. It takes a certain lack of intense interest and expectancy for the phenomena to start. Once they begin, all the fright, apprehension, and every other kind of emotion they engender does not seem to stop them. But watchful waiting seems to be death to any kind of supernormal manifestation.

CHAPTER SIX

Ghosts, Hauntings, and Famous People

"People think ghosts are always evil," says actress Audrey Meadows. "They're not. They can be very nice people."

Audrey should know. She once spent the summer in a haunted room. Attractive, red-haired Audrey is, of course, the well-known comedienne of television and movies who is best known for her role with Jackie Gleason in "The Honeymooners." Her ghost experience occurred the summer she had just turned twenty-one and had landed a part in the singing chorus of a summer-stock musical company in Montclair, New Jersey.

Writing of her experiences in *Fate* magazine, Audrey says that she and a friend named Mary took a room on the second floor of a pleasant, clean, and neat private home. Mary was such a materialist that, according to Audrey, she never knew a thing about the ghost with whom they shared quarters.

The room they occupied had obviously once been used by a child; there were children's books in the bookcase and the lamp on the dresser had nursery-rhyme figures on the shade.

The first night they were there was hot and humid, and

so they opened the window wide before retiring. But when they awakened the next morning, the window was shut tight. This happened regularly after that. At first they joked about it, but soon it was no joke. Audrey felt she had to know what made it happen. The landlady said she had nothing to do with it and had no idea what caused it. They even shoved the dresser in front of the door of their room, in case someone was managing to enter; but the window was closed again the next morning. Of course, there was no mechanical reason by which it could have shut itself. They ascertained that right away.

Another strange thing was that the volume of *Black Beauty* was often pulled out from the bookcase during the night. When replaced on the shelf it was always out again shortly thereafter.

Now, Audrey inherited a very strong psychic sensitivity from her mother. She began to have a feeling she was being watched. Finally, she spoke of this to her landlady, and then she learned the solution to her problem. The lady's twelve-year-old son had died in that room a few years before. He had caught the flu when a draft blew on him from that window during a sudden cold snap—hence his efforts to protect them from the same experience. And his favorite book had been *Black Beauty*. His mother was very pleased when Audrey told her that her son came back at night.

Audrey Meadows stayed in that room all summer and had a very happy time. The ghost was good, sweet, and innocent, and she rather enjoyed his company. "I've had quite a few experiences like this," she says, "but this was one of the nicest."

Dave Garroway, television personality and former host of NBC's "Today Show," had an unseen visitor who was just the opposite. Garroway's six-story house on East 63rd Street, New York City, used to belong to a doctor whose wife was a sister of Rudyard Kipling. Since Garroway has been there his home was, at least for a long period of time, visited by some entity or entities who always opened the doors every night. No matter how carefully they had been bolted, each morning they were found to be unlocked. Garroway told the New York *Post*, "I don't like it, because I don't understand it. It could be dangerous. Maybe next week they'll start a fire and there are three kids in the house." The children were David, Michael, and Paris.

The medium Ethel Meyers once held a seance in Dave Garroway's house and says she learned that an evil old man haunted the place. There has since been a terrible tragedy in this home, and Mrs. Meyers is firmly convinced that the unpleasant old ghost was responsible for it.

Actress Elke Sommer and her husband, writer Joe Hyams, have a ghost at their Beverly Hills, California, home, who has been described as a large, untidy man, full of hate. Clairvoyant Lotte von Strahl says he is also "quite drunk." Joe Hyams wrote the story of their experiences with the ghost for *The Saturday Evening Post*. In it he concludes, "At this point it had been nearly two years since we first heard the sound of furniture moving at night and since the first 'sighting' of a ghost in our house. Thirty-six sensitives, mediums, and investigators have come through our home, and all of them have agreed on at least one conclusion: the house seems to be haunted. More important, we have the independent, detailed, and, I am convinced, completely honest reports of our friends to back up that conclusion."

Other stars have had briefer bouts with the unknown: Actress Olivia deHavilland walked home from a party with a friend whom she hadn't seen for some time and learned the next morning that he had died before the party began. Actress Ida Lupino talked with a ghost on the telephone. She had quite a conversation with a friend of her father's, whose voice she recognized and who spoke to her about things familiar to them both—several days after his death. Actor Jimmie Cagney was warned by the voice of his deceased father to slow down when he was driving too fast. He did, and around the next curve was a stalled trailer in the middle of the road, into which he would have crashed had he not taken his father's advice. Opera singer Patrice Munsel owns a house in Italy where the ghost of a child is reported to walk. Robert Currier, brother of popular singer Jane Morgan, owns a home in Kennebunkport, Maine, which is haunted by a Quaker maid and an unhappy man, who have been dubbed "Ned and Nellie." Both Jane and her mother have heard many strange sounds in this house which have frightened them very much. The wife of the late novelist Kenneth Roberts actually saw the ghosts there.

The Governor of the State of Delaware, the Honorable Charles L. Terry, Jr. lives in a famous haunted house. According to the New York *Times*, "The house is stately old Woodburn, a building of Middle Georgian architecture set in a mellow, tree-shaded residential section of

Dover and complete with many legends about ghosts." It was built in 1790 by Charles Hillyard, whose great-grandfather had been given the land by William Penn. "It has," the report states, "beautifully paneled walls, attractive fireplaces, a boxwood garden, seven bedrooms, a music room, a dining room, a grand hall—and a gloomy cellar."

It is the cellar which is most well known for its haunts, because it was the harbor for runaway slaves during the time when Woodburn was a station on the Underground Railway. One ghost is that of a raider who, seeking to capture the slaves hidden there and sell them back to their owners, climbed into the hollow of an old tulip tree to hide and accidentally hanged himself. The tree still stands on the grounds.

"Another ghost," says the *Times*, "is said to parade about in Revolutionary War costume."

The Terrys have considerable respect for their ghosts.

Troubador-actor Burl Ives is of Scotch-Irish descent, so perhaps that is why he was able to see a ghost at a time when the people he was with were unable to observe it. Ives told his story to columnist Danton Walker, who published it in *Spooks de Luxe*. He said:

"While driving to a house about an hour's ride from Dublin, I was occupying the back seat of a small car. A woman friend was driving and another woman occupied the front seat alongside of her."

About twenty minutes before they reached the house of the hostess with whom they were to dine, Ives noticed a figure standing in the road, directly in the path of the car. In the dusk he could still distinguish that it was a man wearing a large cloak. "Like most back-seat drivers," Ives says, "I was tempted to cry out and warn the driver, but just before we reached the spot where the man had been standing, he disappeared."

He spoke of this curious disappearance to the women in the front seat, but neither of them had seen the man. This, of course, aroused Burl Ives' curiosity, and so he asked his hostess, when they arrived at their destination, and she told him immediately that he had seen an apparition. Many people had seen him just at that spot on the highway, she said.

"Who is it?" asked Ives.

His hostess answered, "It is one of the local legends that St. Kevin sought refuge from the world in a cave near here. A woman found her way to his hiding place and succeeded in making the holy man break his vows and make love to her. St. Kevin was so overcome with remorse—the story goes—that he killed the woman, and then did away with himself by leaping over the stone parapet that borders the road, at the spot where you say you saw the apparition disappear."

Odd that Burl Ives' impression when the apparition disappeared was that it had paused only momentarily in the middle of the road, then had crossed over it to the side that was bordered by a low stone wall, beyond which was a sheer drop. He said, "At the time, it occurred to me that whoever the person was, he was taking quite a chance to attempt to climb down that bank." But if he was a ghost, he could have done it easily. Ghosts, it seems, can do 'most anything.

Vincent Price, "the King of the Ghouls," has considerable evidence from his family history to back up his statement that he believes in ghosts. To admit to such a belief would seem to be good publicity on his part, since his movies are usually of a fiendish or ghastly nature; but he insists that his interest in the subject is based upon reasoning as well as family experience. "I prefer to believe," he wrote "that there are mental powers men have scarcely tapped and little understand."

Price, who is an art collector and critic of national reputation as well as a suave and smooth actor, goes on to tell the story of his young uncle who was killed in a hunting accident, and how his uneasy spirit was comforted. His grandmother was greatly affected by the death of her son, Vincent's father's brother. She took to her room and did not emerge for months. Then, suddenly one evening, she appeared for dinner and joined the family, apparently recovered from her grief. That night, in the drawing room, she quietly rose from her chair, and, as if acknowledging an unseen request, went to the piano, sat down, and played a piece no one had ever heard before. No one had even heard her play before—she did not know a single note of music! When she had finished, she smiled and conversationally thanked her dead son for requesting that piece. She repeated the same performance every night for a week, playing the piano beautifully, always a different tune. Then, on the last night, she spoke once more to her dead boy, thanked him again, and this time said, "Good night, and rest, my dear one, I shan't play for you again."

Price wrote, "This story was told to me as gospel. Those who witnessed the event, while amazed, nevertheless accepted it as a blessing, because it brought the poor lady solace. It cured her grief and, they felt, comforted the young man's spirit and put him to rest."

Rudolph Valentino was probably the greatest matinee idol in history. He and his wife Natacha Rambova were interested in psychic phenomena of all kinds, and Rudy is said to have been deeply psychic himself. His reported experience in a haunted castle would substantiate this rumor.

It was on their honeymoon in Europe that the couple visited the ancient ruins of Locke. Yes, Locke, it says in an article called "Rudolph Valentino—Psychic Genius" by G. B. Chandler in *Orion* Magazine. I know no more about it than that. I don't know where Locke is or how to learn where Locke is. But Chandler says it is an "interesting old castle." Rudy was enchanted with it, and covered it thoroughly. Chandler writes:

"Wandering alone through the ancient dungeons and torture chambers of that great castle he stooped to enter a very low doorway. Suddenly a scream filled with fear and agony pierced the dimly lighted air. In telling of this later Rudy admitted that his blood almost froze in his veins.

"Straightening up he found himself in a room with huge rings and large rusty hooks with chains attached hanging from the walls. In the dim light he could see plainly on the far side of the room the white bones of a human skeleton. Around the skeleton's neck there was a ring. Its arms were outstretched and its bony toes dangled almost to the floor.

"Thinking the skeleton was real, Rudy walked toward it, hoping to see just how it was fastened together. Suddenly the bones vanished, only the empty ring and the old rusty chains remained.

"When Rudy returned to the upper chambers the guide in charge of the castle told him that the room he had been in was formerly a torture chamber. In other centuries he said scores of unfortunates had met violent death in that room. Other victims, he said, had lingered in misery for months, suffering pain and agony beyond belief.

"He added that his wife would never go into that room alone. Like Rudy, the guide's wife was deeply psychic. On many occasions she also had heard that same piercing scream and many times she had seen the same disappearing skeleton."

The new Metropolitan Opera House at Lincoln Center hasn't had time to acquire a haunt in residence yet. But the old Met surely had one, and a good one. It was the wraith of a former opera diva, Mme. Frances Alda. The shade of Mme. Alda was reported frequently to rustle into the operatic audience in a noisy taffeta gown, to thrash about in her seat, to crumple and crinkle her program, all with evident intent of making as much commotion as possible while the soprano on stage was singing. She would hiss, "Flat! Flat!" and nudge whoever happened to be her unfortunate neighbor. (One such operagoer swears her ribs were black and blue from the jabbings.) Since this behavior was typical of the lady after she had retired from her own notable singing career, those who knew her gave her ghost full credit for another remarkable performance. But the specter always disappeared before it could be held accountable.

Best-selling author MacKinlay Kantor, whose *Voice of Bugle Ann* is to me one of the most wonderful books ever written, is rather a hero of mine for that reason. I have also to admire him for the way he handled a haunting experi-

83

ence which would have completely extinguished many people with fright. It occurred in a London rooming house on the night of April 20, 1945, when Kantor was an officer in the U.S. Air Force and stationed in England. Having an evening to spend in London, he found a small unoccupied room in an otherwise crowded home and turned in by 11:00 P.M. He awoke and went down the hall to the bathroom at six minutes after 3:00 A.M., returned to his room, and distinctly recalled hearing the spring lock snap as he closed the door. So when, a short time later, the bed covers began to be pulled off of him, he knew it was not because someone had come into his room. He didn't know what was causing the tugging, but it was no visible body.

Writing in *Fate* Magazine, Kantor says, "I had slept in hundreds of beds in many different countries, but never before had I had an experience like this." The thing that amazed him most was the fact that he didn't feel frightened, merely irritated. Some force was trying to tug the covers from him and Kantor resented that force deeply.

"Four times, when I relaxed my grip, the covers started down again; each time I think it was with greater strength and rapidity." But each of the four times, Kantor grabbed the covers and brought them, the sheet, and comforter back up about his shoulders. Then he came to the conclusion that things had gone far enough. If that force, whatever it was, wanted to get those covers again, it was going to have to take Kantor with them. He dragged the covers up against increasing pressure and locked them tightly about himself. He shoved one side of the comforter under his left shoulder, rolled almost over on his face, jammed more bedclothing in behind him, then rolled back again. In addition, he hung on to the top margin of all three bed garments. The only way the force could drag the covers down now would be by dragging Kantor along with them.

While wrestling with the covers, Kantor began to notice a glow on the east wall. The glow increased in brightness and became somewhat luminescent. In this area of brightness, a form seemed slowly to take shape, as of a head and shoulders, but Kantor could not tell if the shape was a man or woman. As all this activity was going on, sounds began. "Perhaps *a sound* would be more correct. It was more like the murmur of distant voices than anything else I can think of now or could think of then: voices of a number of human beings. Those distant people seemed to be speaking or wailing or laughing rapidly . . . I knew that they were the utterances of human beings, that there were many in number, and that their hullabaloo ran from caterwauling through speechifying and gossip to honest laughter. But I wasn't able to recognize even one word that they were saying."

Kantor was resting mutely all the while, saying to himself: "I won't believe you, I must refuse to look at you, to hear you. I am stronger than you. I will resist. You cannot overcome me. You cannot overcome me. You cannot make me hear or see you."

At that time, Mr. Kantor knew a nominal amount about psychical research but had no interest in haunts. And yet, he instinctively handled this haunt in the most intelligent and successful manner. He refused to look at it and refused to listen to it.

With a heave, he rose to a half-sitting position, still wrapped in the covers, still gripping at them with his hands. He flung himself on his right side, face turned away from the illuminated east wall, and lay with his weight pinioning the crumpled bedclothes on his right side. His left elbow locked a mat of sheet, blanket, and comforter against his body. Kantor was no longer looking at the wall and because of that, he supposes, the voices began to fade. Eventually, he fell asleep.

It had been an hour and a half during which he fought his fantastic opponents; but when he awakened the next morning he had nothing but hands paralyzed from clutching the bedcovers as a souvenir of his experience.

Later, when he was somewhat recovered, Kantor, together with other volunteer researchers, tried to revisit the room for a night, but permission could not be obtained because the house had been turned into a private hostelry for the transient employees of an oil company.

The White House has its quota of haunts, and Abraham Lincoln is the favorite. Among those who have allegedly seen or heard him are Queen Wilhelmina of The Netherlands. When visiting at the White House she opened the door of her room to a strange knock one night and saw Lincoln standing there. The next morning she is said to have told this to Franklin D. Roosevelt who replied that he was not too surprised, because his wife had also felt something strange.

Indeed, Eleanor Roosevelt had mentioned that several times when she was working at her desk in the room that had been Abraham Lincoln's bedroom, she had felt someone behind her. Even when she turned around and saw that no actual phantom was in evidence, she still knew that the unseen presence was there.

Mrs. Coolidge saw the Great Emancipator standing at a window in the Oval Room—that same window where he had so often stood looking out toward Virginia, deeply concerned about the progress of the Civil War. White House servants have also seen him standing there.

When President Harry Truman said that he had heard Lincoln knock on his bedroom door, he was only kidding. He several times heard some kind of an unexplained knock, but he is too much of a materialist to believe that it could have actually been Lincoln's ghost walking the hall. He attributed their cause, instead, to warning signals that parts of the interior of the White House were on the verge of collapse. It will be recalled that it was during Truman's tenure that the structure was completely renovated.

When asked about this, Herbert Hoover said, "I didn't hear any of the sounds in the White House that President Truman heard; but I did hear a lot of others—many of them fantastic."

While Lincoln was probably the most spiritual man ever to inhabit the White House, it is also known that he was quite psychic himself and had several unaccountable experiences of his own, including a dream which presaged his own funeral.

His son Willie Lincoln, who died in the White House, was often seen there as a ghost during President Ulysses S. Grant's administration. But it is the women ghosts in the Executive Mansion who do the most curious things. Dolly Madison is said once to have become quite upset when the second Mrs. Woodrow Wilson ordered her old flower garden dug up. She flounced up to the gardeners in all her ancient finery and told them off in no uncertain terms. Abigail Adams, the wife of the second president of the United States, is said to have been seen also on occasion. What, of all things, was she up to? She was doing her laundry in the East Room!

CHAPTER SEVEN

Haunts Outside of Houses

Houses aren't the only things that can be haunted. Museums, churches, saloons, court houses—most any place may be haunted if enough human emotion has been involved with it. Even a town is haunted—Salem, New York, whose Gray Man has trod its streets for centuries. Not many ghosts have a book dedicated to them, but the Gray Man has.

> To him of airy form, yet venerable mien
> Who, as the 'man in gray,' time and again was seen,
> Though curious strangers for him vainly look
> The History Committee dedicate this book.

The volume with this sentiment is entitled *The Salem Book* and was published in 1896 by a local historical committee. In it are many notes of interest about the early inhabitants of this little village near the Vermont border in Upper New York State, which was founded in 1761 and still retains considerable Colonial charm. One of the prominent citizens of long ago discussed glowingly in this book was General John Williams; although his biographical notes oddly enough do not mention that after his death it was he who became the very "man in gray" to whom the book was dedicated.

There has never been any doubt in the minds of local

townspeople as to the identity of their prominent haunt. He received his sobriquet because whenever he has manifested himself in various streets of the town, he has always been dressed all in gray, and even gray as to face and feature. Those who have claimed to see him—and very few sightings have been reported in recent years, although they used to be a commonplace occurrence—seldom expressed fright or horror. It rather seems that they felt that General Williams' benevolent interest in his old home town is what continues to draw him back.

Salem was actually his adopted home town, for John Williams was born in Barnstaple, England. His birth date is known—1752, but not many details of his early life are recorded. He made medicine and surgery his profession and he came to Salem originally as the town doctor. Called into the army in 1773, he soon, because of his outstanding traits of leadership and his record as a great soldier, went straight to the top. But from where his vast wealth was accumulated it is not known. He probably bought large quantities of land when it was incredibly cheap. Eventually he was reputed to be the richest man in the county. To top that all off, this creature of superlatives was also known as a linguist and one of the most learned men of his time. All these sterling virtues were appreciated, too, by his fellow townsmen. *The Salem Book* says:

"To General Williams and his descendants is the town of Salem largely indebted for her prosperity and growth in the past. His great skill as a lawgiver, his strong and learned mind, his courage on the field of battle, his ability as shown in times of peace all tend to make him one of the most remarkable and prominent men of the Revolutionary epoch."

John Williams died in 1806 at the age of fifty-three. To

have done so much to make his mark on a community in so short a time is slightly spectacular. His influence is everywhere seen, even now. No wonder that he hated to leave for good a town which so revered him. Reports were rather frequent in bygone days that he had *not* left it, that, dressed in his habitual gray costume, he continued to walk or ride up and down the streets and roads so familiar to him.

Those who saw him most often, and about whose experiences the most has been reported, were his two great-granddaughters, both brilliantly educated old maids: Miss Frances (Fannie) and Miss Harriet Martin Williams. They lived all their lives in the magnificent mansion John Williams had built in the center of town. It has recently been torn down and the Salem Central High School built on the property.

Miss Harriet published a book in 1911 called *The Gray Man*. In it she didn't hesitate to say that her great-grandfather's phantom frequently walked into her parlor, surveyed it pleasantly, and then disappeared.

A man who knew these old sisters well is Dr. Adelbert C. Abbott, a retired Syracuse cardiac specialist who has recently returned to Salem to live. He says, "There was a very weighty tradition in the family that the old gentleman was still stirring around." Dr. Abbot and his wife now live on East Broadway, where, for something to do, they run an antique shop. But he was born in the house right next door to the Williams' and used to be great friends with the family. Dr. Abbot says, "The General's picture hanging in the old Williams mansion used to scare the devil out of me." This was because no matter where you were in the room his eyes followed you. A boy couldn't do anything naughty in that house—not with the General's eyes seeing into the depths of his soul.

Times change, and so do legends of the past, "But," Dr. Abbott says, "when I was a kid everybody believed in the Gray Man Ghost." Poor Gray Man. It would be sad to be a benevolent ghost who only wants to do good, and not be believed in.

The haunted museum is in England, and, for a period of several months in the fall of 1953, there was a good bit of activity going on there spookwise. The focal point was a volume entitled *Antiquities and Curiosities of the Church*, edited and published by William Andrews in 1896. That is the kind of a book which ought legitimately to spend its time lying sedately on a library shelf, probably never disturbed by man or ghost. Yet in the Yorkshire Museum in Museum Street, York, England, this book went on monthly personal peregrinations from its shelf to the floor.

It all started when the phantom of a little old gentleman in Edwardian dress appeared to George Leonard Jonas, caretaker of the museum. On Sunday, September 20, 1953, an evangelical meeting was held in the museum. Mr. Jonas and his wife were on duty. Since they did not live at the museum they were not usually there on Sunday evenings, so the ghost may have been wandering about there undiscovered for years. But on this particular night, after the meeting, Mr. Jonas locked the front door and went with Mrs. Jonas into the kitchen, in the basement. From there they both heard footsteps in the Museum above them, so Mr. Jonas went back upstairs to investigate. Here is his own account of what he saw, as told to Brian Lumley of the Yorkshire *Evening Press*:

"I told her it must be Mr. Willmott, Keeper of the Museum, going to his office," Mr. Jonas said. "I went upstairs to tell him we were ready to leave. I fully expected to see him, but when I was halfway up the stairs I saw an elderly man crossing from Mr. Willmott's office into another room. I thought he was an odd looking chap because he was wearing a frock coat, drain pipe trousers and had fluffy side whiskers. He had very little hair and walked with a slight stoop.

"I decided he must be an eccentric professor. As I neared the top of the stairs, he seemed to change his mind, turn, and walk back into the office. When I got to the door, he seemed to change his mind again and turned quickly to come out.

"I stood on one side to let him pass and said, 'Excuse me, sir, are you looking for Mr. Willmott?' He did not answer but just shuffled past me and began to go down the stairs toward the library.

"Being only a few feet from him, I saw his face clearly and could pick him out from a photograph any time. He looked agitated, had a frown on his face, and kept muttering: 'I must find it; I must find it.'

"It was queer, but I did not think about ghosts for one minute. He looked just as real as you or me. But I did not want him roaming around so late at night, and anyway I wanted to lock up and catch my bus.

"As I followed him down the stairs, I noticed he was wearing what seemed to be elastic-sided boots, and I remembered thinking how old-fashioned the big black buttons looked on the back of his coat.

"Still muttering, he went into the library. It was in darkness and I switched on the lights as I followed him in a few yards behind. He was standing between two tall book racks pulling first one book and then another from one of the shelves. He seemed anxious to find something.

"I thought to myself, this has gone far enough. So, thinking he was deaf, I stretched my right hand out to touch him on the shoulder. But as my hand drew near his coat, he vanished and the book he had been holding dropped to the floor."

The book he had dropped was entitled *Antiquities and Curiosities of the Church* and this is the first instance of its unseemly activity.

But not the last.

Mr. Jonas had not been well and this sort of thing was not likely to make him better. He demanded corroborating witnesses to his experience and Mr. Willmott, the Keeper of the Museum, agreed to keep watch with him. As the series of evangelical meetings continued, Willmott stayed with Jonas each Sunday after that for the next three weeks. But nothing happened.

Then on the evening of Sunday, October 18, 1953, shortly after Willmott had left, George Jonas saw the apparition again. It came down the stairs from the first floor, crossed the hall, and passed through the closed library door. The time was 7:40 P.M. The book was not disturbed this time. But Mr. Jonas was.

Since the ghost seemed to have an aversion for Mr. Willmott another friend, Walter French, was asked to keep watch with Jonas, and on the night of November 15 their vigil was rewarded.

In the library, as they walked among the book stacks, they both heard pages of a book being turned. Then they both heard a thud. When they reached the center aisle

93

they discovered this same book, which the ghost had been so eager to find, lying on the floor. Its pages were still in motion. Again it was 7:40 P.M., but this time the ghost himself was not visible.

By now George Jonas was considerably upset. He went to his doctor with his story, fully expecting to be looked at queerly. And he was. His doctor did not admit that his patient could have seen a ghost. And to help prove that he had not the doctor agreed to go to the library with Jonas on the next likely Sunday night.

The pattern for the ghostly visitations appeared to be every fourth Sunday at 7:40 P.M. So on the night of December 13 the doctor, a lawyer and several other persons stationed themselves in the Museum library to wait for the ghost.

As the seven persons present could not all watch the book in question, they scattered throughout the room. They had investigated the book where it lay on its shelf and ascertained that it was not rigged in any way for a trick.

Among the assembled seven was James Lawrence Jonas, George Jonas's older brother, who was an engine-driver by profession. James had scoffed at his brother and said he feared he was going daft. But on this occasion it was James Jonas who saw *Antiquities and Curiosities* in actual flight. He said it seemed to come out its full width from the shelf before it started to fall.

"It didn't seem to fall at the same speed books usually fall," James Jonas reported afterwards.

As he saw the book move he called out and everyone rushed to the spot to find the book lying on the floor, its pages turning. A new examination of the shelf was made.

This time the doctor used a flashlight, but there were no strings or threads or wires to be found.

"I wouldn't have acted for anybody who told me a story like this," the lawyer stated, "but we have the proof of our own eyes."

The doctor admitted that, just before the book moved, his legs, from the knees to his feet, suddenly had felt unusually cold, and that immediately after the book fell his legs returned to normal. "It's incredible," he said. "Without a doubt that book was taken from the shelf by something that is not of this world."

"Maybe somebody will believe me now," George Jonas murmured.

An old Pickens County Negro has identified the face on the Carrollton, Alabama, Court House window as definitely that of Henry Wells. "Yes, sir," he said. "Course I know that face. Didn't I play with him when we were boys, and didn't I see him when they brought him back here all shot to pieces? I'm here to tell you, that picture on the window is the sure 'nough spitting image of old Henry Wells who burnt down the Court House." And anyone in Carrollton will assure you that the face which has somehow managed to engrave itself on the window pane, is really the face of a frightened dark-skinned man. They can see it plainly. For the record, a personal friend of mine, Flint Liddon of Jackson, Mississippi, has seen the face in the window. He also assures me that back of the grimacing depiction on the windowpane, he also saw the actual ghost himself.

History confirms the story of Henry Wells, who burned down the Court House at Carrollton which stood where this one now stands. It was on November 16, 1876, on Thursday morning. He was arrested two years later and died in jail in Carrollton in February, 1878, from the effects of wounds received while attempting to escape. It was in that same month that the Court House windows were put in place. But, you ask, what has that to do with the face in the window?

It is a queer thing that repetition without contradiction often comes to be taken as truth, and in this case a story has been often repeated that it is here set down as at least partly true. So draw near and I will tell it to you as it was told to me.

It is said that when Henry Wells was brought back to Carrollton the citizens of the county were greatly enraged, for he was suspected of other and more serious crimes than that of burning a Court House. To save him from the outraged mob Henry was hidden in the garret of the new Court House. It was then that an electric storm passed over—just when Henry was looking down in terror upon those gathered in the square below—and Henry's face was stamped as indelibly upon that pane as though a photographer had opened his lens and caught the likeness. Whether it is a good likeness of Henry or not may be a matter of some dispute, but it certainly pictures all the emotions the unfortunate Negro must have experienced— horror, sorrow and pain.

And some people say that on stormy nights, when the wind makes weird noises around the eaves of the Court House, one can see by the glare of the lightning the ghost of Henry Wells peering out of the garret window.

Through all the years, in spite of hail and storm which destroyed all the other windows, this particular pane with its striking image remains. It has been scrubbed with soap and rubbed with gasoline by those who doubt its permanence, but it has met every test and the face remains unchanged. At close range this pane is as other panes in the sash, clear and flawless glass. It has to be viewed from the ground—from the spot where once an angry mob gathered—in order for the face to be seen clearly.

A saloon in a 500-year-old inn at Brentwood, England, is haunted. The Swan Inn has been steadily in operation as a hostel all these years, and its ghost is reported to be William Hunter, a Protestant martyr who spent his last night there before going to his death.

The most recent report of supernatural activities in this old inn comes from the summer of 1963, when Mrs. Elizabeth Harding and her twenty-six-year-old daughter Carol took over the management there. After that they were afflicted every night with some kind of manifestations. Carol said, "Religious plates and ornaments fixed to the wall tumble down mysteriously. The saloon doors crash in the night, and my Alsatian dog, Trudy, who has been brought up in bars, refused to sleep there."

When Carol and her mother came down from their rooms each morning they found the saloon door blocked by chairs, which they had heard being dragged across the floor during the night. And lights which they had carefully switched off before retiring were blazing.

"My mother loves it all, but I am quite frightened," Carol Harding told newspaper reporters.

Author Louis Adamic discovered a haunted church near Pittsburgh, Pennsylvania, and has discussed it in several of his writings, introducing it as "The Millvale Apparition." Adamic said his purpose in writing the story was to draw the attention of psychical researchers to the case and to state the facts accurately before the newspapers had the chance to dramatize and distort them. Whether the Millvale apparition has ever been subjected to an acceptable investigation by researchers is not known. The story that Adamic wrote is briefly as follows:

Maxo Vanka, for many years a professor of painting at the Zagreb Academy of Art and a well-known exhibitor in many of the capitals of Europe, came to this country in 1934 to sell some of his work. He is a personal friend of Adamic, who met him in Yugoslavia five years ago. From Adamic's description, Vanka is not only a fine painter, but an interesting and sympathetic character as well. Among other things, Vanka has a remarkable gift with animals who do not appear to fear him at all.

Vanka was rather disappointed with his trip to America until he received a commission from a Croatian church in Millvale, Pennsylvania, near Pittsburgh, to paint a series of murals. Father Zagar, the parish priest, conceived the idea of the murals and interviewed Vanka, giving him carte blanche to paint anything he liked providing religious subjects were included. Vanka was much taken with Father Zagar, whom he found to be an exceptionally sympathetic and intelligent man. Vanka went to see the church and although the curvature of the walls made the task difficult, the other conditions were so ideal that he promised to complete the task in two months.

The town of Millvale is an industrial center, and the church stands high on a hill above railroad yards and factories. The parochial school, which is run by nuns, adjoins the church on one side, and the parish house in which Father Zagar and his assistant, Father Sorich, live, on the other. During Vanka's stay in Millvale, he lived at the parish house and in order to finish such a large commission is so short a time, he worked every night until two or three A.M.

During the hours of work, Vanka requested that no one be allowed to enter the church lest they distract him by talking or fall over the scaffolding. Therefore, Father Zagar kept the church locked from nine in the morning after the last mass until after Vanka had completed his work.

For the first few days nothing untoward happened. Then one night, approximately between the hours of eleven and midnight, Vanka looked down from the scaffold where he was completing a picture of the Madonna, and saw a man, dressed in black, standing before the altar. He thought, of course, that it was Father Zagar, knowing that no one else, except Father Sorich who always retired early, had access to the church. Vanka felt vaguely annoyed as he had requested that he be left undisturbed, but he was so engrossed in his work that he paid no further attention to the figure below him. He noticed that some dogs that slept outside the church were barking excitedly and when he went out about two o'clock, they dashed up to him and licked his hands. However, he thought nothing of it and joined Father Zagar for a cup of coffee before retiring. He immediately became absorbed in general topics and forgot to ask Father Zagar what he was doing before the altar so late at night.

The following night Vanka noticed nothing and by contrast with the previous night, the dogs were quiet. On the eighth night however, looking down from the scaffold he saw the same figure, and again supposing it to be Father

Zagar, paid little attention. He noticed that the man was making queer gestures, however, and wondered why Father Zagar should be practicing rituals at that time of night. A little later, he heard "him" walking down the aisle of the church. Meanwhile the dogs were barking once more. When he returned to the parish house later, he found Father Zagar asleep on the couch. As he awoke, Father Zagar exclaimed "Why didn't that woman wake me?" meaning his housekeeper. He explained that he had told her when he lay down at nine o'clock to wake him at eleven, but she had evidently fallen asleep herself.

Vanka was naturally puzzled but concluded that Father Zagar must be a somnambulist. Vanka questioned him about it and Father Zagar grew very serious asking why Vanka should want to know. Vanka told him what he had seen in the church. Zagar assured him that he never walked in his sleep and said that he had definitely been asleep on the couch throughout the evening. He then asked if Vanka had heard the tradition that the church was sometimes visited by a ghost. Vanka had never heard it. Father Zagar then related the fifteen-year-old tradition that the church was haunted at night occasionally and the ghost had been seen by several members of the parish. It was thought that the ghost was a former priest of the parish who had not performed his duties properly and was now making up for his misdemeanors. A predecessor of Father Zagar had left on the ghost's account, but Father Zagar himself had never seen anything. He then admitted that he had been staying up every night until Vanka had finished, lest he should have some such experience and fall off the scaffold or otherwise be frightened.

Vanka thought perhaps Father Zagar was a little crazy but the impression of the figure remained. After that

Father Zagar came into the church and helped Vanka mix his paints until the work was finished for the night. The following night, he came into the church at a quarter to eleven. He jokingly asked the ghost to come out and show himself exclaiming that he was not afraid of him. Soon after there was a strange click in a corner of the church which sent a chill through Vanka. Father Zagar suggested it was the scaffolding which constantly creaked, but this was a different sound. Another click of a mysterious kind sounded in another corner. Father Zagar stood on one side of the altar and spoke in a sharp voice:

"Come on, show yourself if you are a ghost or whatever you are; or speak if you can. We're busy here, the *Gospodiné professor* and I, decorating the church, making it beautiful, and we should like to be left alone. If you're a ghost, if you're a dead man, go with God—peace to you. I'll pray for you. Only please don't bother us—"

Vanka interrupted him with a yell, "for just then I saw him—the ghost; or at least, let me call him that—sitting in the fourth pew. I saw him very clearly: a man in black, an old man with a strange angular face wrinkled and dark with a bluish tinge. He leaned on the front part of the pew, looking up—not so much at me as at everything in general: a sad, miserable gaze. I saw him for just a moment, then—nothing. He vanished. But I felt cold all over at the same time that sweat broke out of every pore of my body. I got off the scaffold, which wasn't high for that mural, and barely managed not to fall off the ladder, I was so frightened. . . . Father Zagar, who followed me out, had not seen the ghost and, taking the attitude of the skeptic again, he said I had probably only imagined I saw him."

For some nights afterwards peace reigned and then the

ghost was seen again: "There was that strange awful knock or click in one corner under the choir, then another in the other corner. 'O-ho,' cried Zagar, scratching his head. I used up what paint I had in the pail, then laid everything aside and got off, intent on fleeing, for I was abruptly all cold inside and beginning to drip with perspiration. But the Father detained me, seizing my arm, suggesting we face the situation. . . . Then I saw him—the old man in black—moving down the aisle altarward. Terrified, horror-stricken, panicky are faint words to describe my sensation. 'Look, Father,' I yelled, 'there he goes—to the altar—he's at the altar—*he's blown out the light!*' "

The light was the sanctuary lamp which is never extinguished and which no breeze can reach. Father Zagar again saw nothing but he rushed to the altar and found the light out and the wick still smoking. Vanka left the church and found the dogs outside yelping at the top of their lungs. Father Zagar followed Vanka out and said:

"Till now, I still had a glimmer of doubt. I thought possibly it was your fantasy, I thought possibly I had imagined the knocks in the church and by my bed the other night. But now I believe. *Bomé*, now I believe. There is something here. That light was blown out just when you said it was."

There are other details which unfortunately cannot be related here. Adamic went to Millvale and talked to others who knew of the ghost. Father Zagar and the housekeeper confirmed every word of Vanka's in telling the story. The ghost continued to appear to Vanka while he finished the work. The organ, an electric one, not susceptible to outside vibrations caused by rumbling lorries, etc., sometimes pealed a single note. At one time, the ghost came earlier than eleven o'clock and Vanka saw him lighting the candles before the altar. Father Zagar found them burnt and testified that no one except Vanka himself, *or the ghost,* could have burnt the candles, because the church was locked.

Adamic suggests the usual theories of subconscious creation in the mind of the artist and of hallucination due to overwork and lack of sleep. But, in that case, who blew out the sanctuary lamp?

The spirits of ancient monks who still haunt their haunts of yore—the demolished Glastonbury Abbey—were responsible for locating the ruins of two of the abbey's buried chapels. Archaeologists did not take too kindly to the report of spirit help, and refused to admit that it had been possible. Some clergymen were simply furious! But Frederick Bligh Bond, the ecclesiastical architect who was director of excavations at Glastonbury Abbey, was tremendously grateful when automatic writing from the old monks made his work easier.

The first abbey building on those hallowed grounds had existed long before history began in England. A little wattle church is said to have been built there in the first century by St. Phillip, the Apostle, and his followers. In the year 166 this wattle church was restored by missionaries sent from Rome at the request of King Lucius. Rumor even has it that the legendary King Arthur was buried somewhere on the abbey grounds. The lost Loretto Chapel —the one which was located for Bond in 1917 by the early monks—was erected by Abbot Richard Beere after his return from Italy in 1503. He had been sent to Rome by King Henry VII to congratulate the new Pope, Pius III, on his election.

Then history had to contend with King Henry VIII and his desire for numerous legal wives. The Catholic clergy became *persona non grata* in England, and Henry went to no end of trouble to make this evident. The last abbot of Glastonbury Abbey—Richard Whiting—a tired, old man whose only offense had been trying to protect the property in his charge, was executed by Henry's order on November 15, 1539. His body was quartered and his head was placed on the abbey gate. All the buildings were later destroyed completely. Rather extreme measures indeed.

In 1908 Frederick Bligh Bond, a member of the Somerset Archaeological Society and a church architect of some repute, was given the job of excavating the ruins of Glastonbury Abbey. During that same period, he and a friend, John Alleyne, were attempting automatic writing at home in their spare time; and they began to receive communications relating to Bond's work at the monastery. The scripts were stated to be written by several of the monks who during one century or another had lived at the abbey. Apparently they still remained at the site, or at least maintained a warm regard for the locale with which they had been most involved during their earthly lives.

Bond and Alleyne worked as a team to receive the automatic writing. Alleyne held the pencil, which lay on large sheets of writing paper. Bond turned the pages when they were filled with writing, and he put his right hand lightly on the back of Alleyne's hand which held the pencil. This acted as a battery, adding power and making reception easier.

The early residents of the abbey seemed delighted with

the opportunity to make their continued presence known and to have the chance to chat about numerous subjects of interest to them. They discussed the buildings as they had been in early days, but they also were happy to palaver about other completely irrelevant topics. The various ones who communicated revealed their disparate personalities, and some of their varied experiences during their lives on earth. There were some who wrote in modern English, but many used mediaeval English, and some spoke in a monkish type of Low-Latin. Even the handwriting changed as different entities wrote; and charming personal gossip about their days at the monastery was frequently given.

Johannes Bryant particularly enjoyed telling about his life on earth. He described himself as a fat, jolly nature lover who had liked to wander away from the abbey to fish in the mere. "And," he said, "the abbot winked at it for he knew full well that it was good for me." Johannes said there were 347 people in the monastery when he lived there and that he "didde sleepe on the south side, hard by the great gabell where at night the sound of many waters refreshed ye parched soil. From tower and from high roofes the sound came like the sound of waterfloods."

When Bond tried to get the writing down to the case at hand and asked for specific information about the location of certain buildings on the abbey property, he received specific answers. A communicant who signed himself Camillus Thesiger and said that he had been a man named Camel who was the Treasurer for Abbot Beere, gave considerable worthwhile advice. He recorded the specific location and dimensions of the abbey's Edgar Chapel, and when Bond went out and dug where he was told, he discovered the ruins of the Edgar Chapel in that very spot. After finding this as directed by automatic writing, Bond published the fact—receiving nothing but scorn for his effort. Nobody would believe he hadn't located the chapel first and then for some crazy reason made up the story about how he got the information.

Bond did not give up his interest in excavating at Glastonbury Abbey, and decided to concentrate on trying to find the Loretto Chapel. He believed that it had once existed because there was a reference in Leland's sixteenth century chronicle which stated that there had been a Loretto Chapel "joining to the north body of the church." With this sole bit of information to guide him, Bond dug outside the north wall of the church in 1911; but he found no trace of walling or foundation trenches, and the search was finally abandoned. Obviously he did better when guided by the ghostly handwriting.

For five years no further efforts were made to find the Loretto Chapel. Then one day Frederick Bligh Bond ran into John Alleyne again, and they decided to try to do some more automatic writing together. On December 4, 1916, they began a new series of correspondences with the spirit world, and right away Thesiger began to wield the pencil. When told that Bond wished to try to locate the Loretto Chapel, Thesiger told him that it was 31½ feet away from the church. This surprising information was in sharp contradiction to Leland's statement that the chapel adjoined the church. Thesiger wrote that when Bond had tried to find the chapel in 1911 he had not gone far enough beyond the "bank." This bank was mentioned again during an automatic writing session on August 16, 1917. The communicator said that deep by the bank was the wall where the fathers used to sit in their old age. The destroyers of the abbey had covered this wall at the west end of the Loretto Chapel with dirt to make a bank six feet high. By doing this they had saved the wall "for all tyme," according to Thesiger. He also said that the chapel was "40 feet by 20 feet or thereabouts." With these clues to go on, Bond felt that he might now find the Loretto Chapel if he started to dig. Profiting by experience, he knew enough to publish his scripts first in order to have proof later in case they turned out to be accurate. His book *The Gate of Remembrance* thus came out long before he ever put a shovel to the earth in his Loretto Chapel search.

And so when he began digging operations into the bank in August, 1919, he had already published the account of what Thesiger had told him to expect to find, and where. And he did find the chapel exactly there. In less than two hours the shovelers encountered masonry, and the following day they uncovered a well-built foundation of rough stonework forming the southwest corner of a building. When the work was finished, the only perfect foundation remaining of the entire chapel was the west wall — the one their communicant had said was saved "for all tyme."

By the time cold weather ended the 1919 digging season, Bond had sufficient data to draw a diagram of the whole chapel. The next summer the work was finished, revealing that exactly what the automatic writing had said about the location of the building was true. No living person had known anything about where these old buried remains could be found. But the monks who used to live there did, and they didn't hesitate to say so explicitly when given the opportunity to communicate.

CHAPTER EIGHT

Haunted Ships

Many tall tales of terror come from the sea, and not the least of these are the stories of haunted ships. Seldom are they supported by any evidence, but they make good listening, anyway.

One yarn which is quite old, but which at least offers an identity for the ghost, comes from George Little, who wrote a book called *Life on the Ocean; or Twenty Years at Sea*, published in 1843. He says that he was on a brig which sailed from Baltimore, Maryland, on March 11, 1817, for the West Indies with a crew of ten men and a boy plus the captain.

The shipboard shenanigans began one beautiful night when the brig was anchored out from Annapolis. Members of the crew were sitting on the deck when suddenly one of them pointed silently, his mouth gaping open. The others, looking where he indicated, saw a woman standing there. They all sat on that starlit deck on the silent sea and stared, for they suspected that they must be seeing a ghost. Flesh and blood females seldom popped up on their decks when they were at sea. Finally someone managed to force himself to move, and went for the captain. But neither the captain nor the mate could see her; and soon she disappeared from the view of the others as well. Then they knew for sure that they had seen an apparition, and tradition had it that this boded evil. The men began to mutter among themselves about the wisdom of leaving the ship while there was still time, before they got out on the open sea. But the captain would not hear of it.

Some days later they were standing down the Chesapeake Bay when the phantom appeared again, and very shortly thereafter a terrible storm hit and the ship was almost lost. At Guadaloupe the lady was seen on the forecastle by two of the crew and after that six sailors on the vessel, including the mate, were seized with yellow fever and dysentery. All but one recovered, and since the haunt appeared no more, gradually fear of her diminished.

Why would a mysterious woman haunt the ship? It turned out that there had been a reason. When the brig had sailed from Baltimore the wife of the captain was living in Nantucket. On his return to port at the end of the trip a letter awaited him telling him that she had died suddenly at the very time when the apparition was first seen on board while the craft was lying in Annapolis Roads.

Sometimes ships which acquire the reputation for being haunted have to be destroyed, for it is impossible to get men who will sail on her. The *Pontiac* was such a vessel, a barque which plied her trade between Liverpool and South America. According to an account in *News of the World*, March, 1864, the *Pontiac* put into Callao, Peru, in July, 1863, where her captain, being short-handed because of the desertion of several of his crew, engaged some new seamen for the voyage home. Among them were Robert Campbell, George Williams, and an Ionian sailor named Jean Moryatos. The *Pontiac* then shipped a load of guano and sailed for Liverpool.

It was not long after the ship had left Callao that the steersman had a bad fright one night. He shrieked to the mate, who was the only other man on deck with him.

"What's the matter?" answered the mate, gruffly, but the steersman could do nothing but gibber and point. Finally he got his voice and gasped, "It's a man, but none of the crew. Can't you see him?" The mate could not. However, as the other insisted, he began to feel creepy. "What's he like?" he asked. "He's a stranger—yes, he's turning his face toward me, I can see it plainly now. Owwww, oh, my God!" The seaman was beside himself.

So was the mate by now. "What, what do you see?" he barked.

"Oh, thank God he's gone," sighed the steersman, finally, sitting down on a piled-up rope because of his quivering knees.

Eventually the mate got from him a description of what he had seen—and it was not pleasant. The face of the stranger, which had been revealed when it had turned and looked directly at the steersman, was that of a skeleton. "Only, there was something in its eye sockets that shone like . . . like very wicked eyes."

The story of the death's-head spread like wildfire, and before daylight all on board were discussing it. Some of the crew laughed and poked fun at the steersman, while others declared their belief in what he said, and expressed their opinion that the ship was haunted and that certain noises which had been recently heard and attributed to rats were really due to the ghost. That night a boy, who had come on board as a stowaway but had been taken on as a hand, was awakened by a sharp tug on the shoulder. He looked around and saw a tall figure, draped from head to foot in black, standing by his side. He was too alarmed to cry out and watched it cross over to the hammock of Robert Campbell, and after pausing there for a few seconds, walk along with long, raking strides to the hammock of George Williams. After a momentary halt there too, it stalked to the entrance of the forecastle, whence it turned and, confronting the stowaway, slowly pushed back the hood that concealed its face. The moonlight, pouring down the open hatch on to it, revealed a grinning death's-head. For some seconds, the stowaway was too petrified to do anything. When at last his faculties returned, the figure was gone. But the boy was screaming in fright. No one in the forecastle slept any more that night, and the following day the ghost's second appearance was the sole topic of conversation.

Campbell laughingly told the stowaway, when several of the men were standing in a group on the main deck, that he intended sharpening his sheath knife, so as to have it ready for the ghost. "If it comes near me tonight," he said, "I will stab it like this," and he made a vicious jab in the direction of Jean Moryatos, who jumped back in a manner that made everyone present roar with laughter. Jean was a sullen, morose fellow, who knew very little English and was universally disliked on board. That evening it was his turn to be on deck.

The crew who were off duty had announced their intention of sitting up to watch for the ghost, but all went to sleep, with the exception of Williams, who lay in his hammock reading. He was far too engrossed in his book to hear stealthy footsteps come creeping down the forecastle ladder and into the forecastle itself. The footsteps were made by a figure who held in one hand a knife with a keen edge that gleamed wickedly in the moonlight. Walking on tiptoe so as not to make a sound, the figure stole up to the hammock of Campbell. Leaning over him, it raised the knife aloft and then plunged it into the sleeping man.

The groan Campbell uttered caused Williams to drop his book and look round, but before he could realize what had happened the figure was on him, and the knife again flashed through the air. It would have descended a second time had not some of the other men sprung out of their hammocks and come to the rescue. A desperate struggle ensued, but in the end the assailant was overpowered. He proved to be Moryatos.

In his defense he declared that he thought Campbell and Williams meant to kill him: that was why Campbell had made a lunge at him with the knife that morning. He said both those men had treated him very badly during the voyage. He was put in irons at once. Campbell died very shortly and Williams soon afterwards. Some of the crew declared now that the ghosts of both these men haunted the ship, and quoted the well-known old sailors' superstition that one ghost on a ship brings another. All kinds of alarming noises were heard during the night and sometimes during the day as well; and when the *Pontiac* arrived at Leith, where Moryatos was handed over to the local police (he was subsequently proved to be insane), a new crew had to be sought for, as none of the old hands would sail in her again.

Whether or not any of the new crews ever actually saw

ghosts aboard her, the ship's reputation was so evil that many fanciful individuals insisted they did; and eventually the owners gave up trying to get anybody to sail on her and broke up the ship and sold it for timber.

Another haunted ship of the last century, the *Hascall*, which was written up in *Harper's* Magazine, September, 1880, was a Maine fishing schooner. During a gale off St. George's Sound she broke loose from her moorings and ran into another ship named the *Andrew Johnson*. The *Hascall* was badly damaged, but the *Andrew Johnson* was hurt even worse, and she soon sank. Now the law of the sea is a law of fair play, and no reputable captain would sail away from a vessel in distress—especially when his own ship had been responsible for the plight. But the *Hascall* at once put into port, making no attempt even to pick up the drowning crew of the other schooner.

From then on the *Hascall* had no peace. That very night people on the wharf alongside her saw queer bluish lights aboard her, when no one was actually on board. As the puzzled loungers on the quay watched, they saw figure after figure come to the side of the vessel and lean over, and act as if they were hauling in a net. Spectral lights hovered over the figures, showing their faces, which were recognized by those on shore as the drowned crew of the *Andrew Johnson*. These phantoms worked for a while where they were, then moved to the other side of the *Hascall* and were seen clambering over the side. Then the sound of oars was heard rowing out to sea, and after that all was still. Especially still were the stunned loungers on the wharf who had been witnessing the event.

But when the shock of what they had seen wore off,

they could talk of nothing else. Every night after that the dock swarmed with people who watched—as the identical scene was reenacted on the *Hascall*—repeatedly for months. Is it any wonder that, when this boat was finally ready to go back to sea, no fishing crew was found who would board her?

Quite often the report of a haunting on a ship is the portent of disaster, not necessarily because of reluctant crews, but because the ghost apparently knows that the vessel is doomed and comes to give the warning. Two men fell from the topmast of a lake vessel with no apparent cause, and were killed, according to the Chicago *Times*, March, 1885. The crew immediately conceived the idea that the ship was unlucky and that there was some presence on board that was antagonistic to them. They behaved quite well, however, till the vessel reached Buffalo, when they refused to sail in her again, on the plea that she was haunted. A new crew was accordingly engaged. While the men were at work discharging the cargo, they got to know of the recent tragedy on board and why the former crew had left. Some of the grain-trimmers at once quit work and said they would have nothing more to do with such a ship. Other men were, with difficulty, prevailed upon to take their place. The day for the entire crew to come on board, prior to sailing, arrived. They arrived, some of them half drunk, and were following the mate to the forecastle, when one of them halted and pointing aloft said, "What have you got that figurehead on the mast for?"

The mate looked up, turned deadly pale, and exclaimed,

"Why, it's Bill!" Bill was one of the men who had fallen from the topmast and been killed.

A panic at once ensued, and mate and men bolted from the ship *en masse* and refused to enter her again. Despite warnings from those who knew what had happened, the captain got a new crew and sailed in the ship, his destination Cleveland. He never got there, however, for his ill-omened vessel was sunk in a collision and he and his crew were drowned.

Sometimes ships don't just lose their crews by default, they lose themselves. There are a number of such authenticated instances which are completely unaccountable in any possible way. During the year 1921, for instance, twelve vessels completely vanished without a trace, and almost simultaneously.

One of the first large ships to vanish at sea was the *President,* sailing from New York on March 11, 1841. No word was ever received concerning the ship or any of the 136 who perished. In 1854, 450 persons disappeared with the *City of Glasgow.*

Tom H. Inkster, writing in the *National Fisherman,* tells of the haunting fascination related to the sudden disappearance of a ship that leaves no trace of its sinking nor any apparent reason for the loss.

"Even in wartime," Inkster says, "it is hard to understand how a staunch ship like the *Cyclops* could vanish without leaving something floating around to mark her sinking."

The *Cyclops* was bound from Barbados, West Indies, to Hampton Roads, Virginia, on a routine voyage. She was in communication with U.S. stations all along the way, when suddenly she either split up or sank. No trace of her, her cargo, or the 309 persons aboard her were ever found, and since the date of March 18, 1918, the disappearance of the *Cyclops* has remained a complete mystery.

Sometimes, Tom Inkster says, these disappearances can turn into a recurring mystery. The fate of the Hudson's Bay Company steamship *Baychimo* is an excellent example. En route to Vancouver, B.C. from the Arctic in a desperate race against the formation of winter ice, the *Baychimo* lost. It was not an easy decision to abandon a ship loaded with valuable furs, but there was no other choice. Off Point Barrow, Alaska, the crew was forced to abandon her as an ice-locked impossibility.

"Weeks later," according to Inkster, "a party of Eskimo seal hunters sighted her but, when her crew arrived, she suddenly vanished.

"Several years later, the *Baychimo* was sighted again. As the American ship *Northland* drew closer to the luckless vessel, a dense fog covered them. When the fog lifted, the *Baychimo* had gone with it."

The White Star steamship *Naronic* disappeared in February of 1893 with seventy-five men on board. In September of 1943, on a trip of only forty miles from Liverpool to Preston, Lancashire, with a load of woodpulp and a crew of nine, the 200-ton steamer *Speke* disappeared and left no trace. If a ship just sank in bad weather, there would almost invariably be bodies washed ashore, debris left from the wreckage, or at least objects from the ship which floated to the surface. But when ghosts capture a ship and sail it away into the unknown it is gone for good and not one spar or spanker of it is left.

About twenty years ago, the *Hopestar* left Newcastle, England, bound for Philadelphia. Somewhere in the mid-Atlantic, the stout ship vanished with forty persons aboard. The British Ministry of Transport concluded that the ship had broken in two or struck a mine but, according to Tom Inkster, sailors shook their heads over the suppositions. "There was no sign of wreckage. Not even one small splinter was ever found afloat or washed up on some beach. So the *Hopestar* became another ghost ship, with seamen wondering if she sank or joined the host of hulls wandering over the seas and popping to the surface in the most unexpected places."

Seamen have always had superstitions about ghosts and ghost ships, the most famous case of fascination in this area being the famed *Flying Dutchman*. Because of an unspeakable blasphemy he uttered, the skipper of this ship is fated to sail until the end of time, in a futile effort to reach the Cape of Good Hope.

Although this story is over three hundred years old and supposedly a legend, modern ships report sightings of the *Flying Dutchman* to this very day. One example is the case of the officers aboard *H.M.S. Bacchante*, including one officer who was later to become King George V. These men are convinced they saw the phantom ship, cruising southern waters.

Reports of phantom ships abound. Here's a case where modern automation may have prevented additional sightings. Tillamook Rock lighthouse was the main guardian beacon to the mouth of the Columbia River. While it was still manned, the crew saw a ghost ship immediately below the rock. Watching the ship in utter amazement, the men

117

saw it disappear into the fog, never to be seen again . . . unless the ship feels more comfortable in the presence of an electric timer.

Another phantom ship may have been the victim of ghosts or even worse. The mystery of the *Marie Celeste*, an American brigantine, has never been solved. Found afloat about 300 miles west of Gibralter, everything aboard the *Marie Celeste* was in order. The decks were neatly scrubbed, the ropes were coiled and in place, bunks were all made, and the table was set for service with dishes, silver, and food. But the ship's log showed no entries having been made for the preceding ten days.

All indications pointed to a vanishing into thin air of the captain, his wife, their young daughter, and a seven-man crew.

There were no signs of mutiny or violence, although one of the small boats was missing. But if they fled the ship, why? Where did they go? And what happened to them? No one knows.

The *Rosalie*, a large French vessel, was found in 1840 in a similar condition. All sails were set, the weather was calm, there was a valuable cargo. Yet every living soul, except for a canary, had disappeared without a trace. The canary is good evidence that some strange unknown poisonous chemical had not disposed of all life on board. But I don't know what else it proves.

The name *Carol Deering* has enchantment as another of those fantastic crafts which were abandoned by all hands for no apparent reason. It went ashore off the coast of North Carolina, and when it was boarded later not one living being was discovered. They had all apparently run off just as a meal was about to be served. In case the idea of some sea monster appeals to you as having reached its slimy tentacles on board and lifted off all members, one by one—the ship was in first-class order. Not even a chair was overturned.

Of course, ships like the *Flying Dutchman* are ghosts because they have no physical form—they are phantoms. But I think these derelicts are ghost ships too. Somehow, for some unknown reason, they suddenly became inhabited by ghosts instead of living human beings. Why, I don't know. I only hope I learn the answers to some of these intriguing questions before I die. Or afterward.

CHAPTER NINE

The Case of the Haunted Girl

In Amherst, Nova Scotia, Canada, in 1879 a girl named Esther Cox was so badly haunted that her life was hardly worth living. Many of the phenomena she experienced were similar to poltergeist activity, but in this instance Esther said she could actually see the ghosts who were tormenting her. When something like the following happened, those around her were inclined to go along with her theory:

One day Esther told her married sister, Olive Teed, that the ghost named Maggie Fisher was wearing her black and white striped stockings.

"Take off my stockings this very instant, you naughty ghost," she said. And immediately the black and white stockings dropped from the air in the middle of the room to the floor—with no one anywhere near them. No one in the flesh, that is. Olive Teed and a boarder named Walter Hubbell were just innocent bystanders, but they saw the stockings materialize—and they believed in ghosts after that.

Walter Hubbell later wrote a book about Esther Cox's experiences, calling it *The Great Amherst Mystery: A True Narrative of the Supernatural*. He was a well-known actor of his day, descended from a respected American family dating back to the Revolutionary War. When his troupe had played in Amherst and he heard about the curious haunting of this girl, he had decided to return after his Nova Scotia tour was completed and try to capitalize on her notoriety. He had planned to exhibit her in theatres as the greatest wonder of the nineteenth century, hoping that the poltergeist activity would continue while she was on stage and he was lecturing about her. At that time he was certain that her claims were a fake, and he intended to make the most of it financially before others learned "how she did it."

Hubbell felt himself to be particularly competent to investigate a haunting because he had no belief in spirits and had already debunked several well-known "mediums." As an actor he felt he had had ample experience, as he put it, with "all those mechanical devices which we use upon the stage, for the presentation of illusive effects so often the wonder and admiration of the public. Possessing this knowledge, gained by years of experience, and being familiar with the methods and paraphernalia used by the magicians in their exhibition of legerdemain, I am, beyond doubt, competent to judge whether there was or was not deception of such kind in the house where I beheld such wonders."

"Truth," he states without too much originality, "is often stranger than fiction. What I have written is the truth, and not fiction, and it is *very strange*. I have not permitted my imagination to so embellish the account as to distort it, nor in any way endeavored to make it attractive at the expense of veracity."

Despite these protestations, one feels inclined to doubt

what seem to be his wilder flights of fantasy. Yet, a signed and notarized letter is appended to the text, in which Olive Teed states that what he has said "is all true." An additional document, notarized and signed by sixteen townspeople, reads:

"Having of our own personal knowledge, and not by or through hearsay or belief, absolutely known, seen, and heard individually all or some of the demonstrations, manifestations, and communications of an invisible, intelligent, and malicious power within the atmosphere that continued its awe-inspiring and mysterious operations in the home of Daniel Teed, 6 Princess Street, Amherst, Nova Scotia, and elsewhere in the actual presence of his sister-in-law, Esther Cox . . . for the period of one year from 1878 to 1879, as narrated by Walter Hubbell . . . which account having been read by us and being known to us as accurate and truthful as to all and each fact, particulars and description given in the aforesaid book, we hereto, of our own free will, affix our names to this testamentary paper so that it may be printed . . . and go before the world in corroboration and verification of what actually transpired in the presence of the Teed family . . ."

So, with these witnesses to corroborate Mr. Hubbell's account, we may, at least for now, take it at face value as we continue with the narrative of events.

The phenomena began in January, 1879, in the home of Daniel Teed, a foreman of the shoe factory in Amherst, a small town near Halifax, Nova Scotia. Besides his wife, Olive, and two quite small sons, Daniel had under his roof his wife's two sisters, Jennie and Esther Cox. Jennie was a pretty and popular twenty-two year old; her younger sister was low in stature and rather inclined to be stout.

Arthur Davison, Clerk of the County Court, for whom she later worked, describes Esther thus: "She was not good looking, very ignorant, only a common education, could read and write but not spell." (He also adds that "I may say in passing I read the book published by Hubbell, and while he painted the facts up to make the book sell, the facts were there all the same.") Davison also said of Esther that, "I have often watched her to find out how she came down stairs, she seemed to fly."

The strange activities, as related by Hubbell, started gently at first, merely as a rustling in a box under the bed. The two girls, who slept together, thought it was caused by a mouse. The second night the rustling increased, so that they pulled the box out from under the bed, and then shrieked for help as the box began to jump. Before the eyes of the assembled family it jumped as high as three feet into the air.

A few evenings later Esther leaped out of bed crying, "My God! What is the matter with me? I'm dying!" Then, as reported by thespian Hubbell, she cried, "I'm swelling up and shall certainly burst, I know I shall." And swollen she was, according to witnesses. While the family stood looking at her, wondering what to do to relieve her, a loud pounding sound was heard in the room. Esther's condition eased, and she went to sleep. (This happened again about four nights later, and intermittently for the rest of the year.)

Next morning, Daniel went for the doctor, and it is well that he did, for we now have on record a letter by the physician, which told of his experiences with the girl. Thomas W. Carritte, M.D., told Daniel he would call in the evening and remain until the following morning, if necessary; but did not hesitate to say that what Daniel told him was all nonsense, and that no such tomfoolery would occur while he was in the house.

Yet the tomfoolery appeared before his eyes. Esther's pillow was pulled from beneath her head and blown up by some invisible force so strong that nobody was able to hold it down beneath her head. The bed clothes flew off the bed, and Esther's physical condition of swelling and pain began just as it had previously. As the doctor puzzled over her condition, loud rappings sounded from beneath the bed, and her torment was relieved.

Dr. Carritte wrote in 1883 to a Professor Rufus D. Pease of Philadelphia, Pennsylvania, as follows:

"I take my pen in hand at this comparatively late moment to say that what Mr. Walter Hubbell has published about the mysterious Esther Cox case is entirely correct, as doctors not only, but clergymen, editors, and perhaps hundreds of other persons from their own independent observations could testify. The young lady was a patient of mine previous to and during those wonderful demonstrations and, with all the rest, I must acknowledge that I was sorely puzzled. I tried various experiments, but with no satisfactory results. I even had her placed on a thoroughly insulated bed, in the center of the room, with reference to possible electric currents, but in vain.

"Honestly skeptical persons were on all occasions soon convinced that there was no fraud or deception in the case. It would take me an entire week to write you a full history of my connection with those strange doings. Were I to publish the case in the medical journals, as you suggest, I doubt if it would be believed by physicians generally. I am certain I could not have believed such apparent miracles had I not witnessed them."

Many other people saw Esther while she was suffering as she had the first night Dr. Carritte was called. Arthur Davison said, "When I saw her, she was on a cot bed, and seemed to be dead, but for a violent heaving of her body, that is from her breast down to her legs, she would fill up and lift the clothes as you inflate a bladder and then it would suddenly collapse. Those spells came in regular order, about every minute."

But to get on to the other manifestations. While Dr. Carritte was there on his first visit, and while he and the rest of the family were in the room, "the bedclothes flew off again; and before they had been put back on the bed to cover Esther, the distinct sound as of some person writing on the wall with a metallic instrument was heard. All looked at the wall whence the sound of writing came, when, to their great astonishment, there could be plainly read these words, 'Esther Cox, you are mine to kill.' " The writing was deeply indented in the wall and looked as if it had been written with a dull instrument.

This was the first indication that an "intelligence" was back of the Amherst mystery. As Dr. Carritte stood in the door wondering what it all meant, a large piece of plaster came flying from the wall of the room, turning a corner in its flight, and fell at his feet. And then the pounding began once again, shaking the room.

The next night when this pounding recurred, the doctor went outside the house, where he heard the sounds in the open air . . . it seemed as if some person were on the roof with a heavy sledge hammer, although in the moonlight he could see no one there. The pounding sounds now commenced in the morning and were heard all day. They were investigated by the preachers of the local churches, who became convinced there was no way for Esther herself to be accomplishing this feat.

Soon Esther began to hear a voice which told her it was that of a man who had once lived on earth, but had been dead for some years. Her family laughed when she told them this, for they said there were no such things as ghosts. But later the girl claimed to be able to see the ghosts. There were several of them, she said, but the two ring-leaders were "Bob Nickel" and "Maggie Fisher." Well, if they were ghosts, they certainly set about proving themselves to be among the most obnoxious ghosts in history. They began setting fires all over the house. These fires flamed up when Esther had been under constant observation by members of her family. But since she was obviously responsible, whether consciously or not, it was decided that she should be sent away before the house burned down.

The poor girl was taken in by a Mr. John White and his wife, who soon began to feel apprehensive when their furniture started to travel about of its own accord. Mr. White ran a restaurant, where Esther helped him. Business became especially good, as people came in to see what strange new manifestations would take place each day.

And now Walter Hubbell enters into the story, for his lecture tour began at this time. He and Esther and John White performed for a short time in neighboring towns. Unfortunately (the ghosts later explained), Esther was so afraid on the stage that she didn't generate enough power for them to perform their antics, so the shows were a flop.

They soon gave up the struggle, returned to Amherst, and Esther went back to her sister's home.

One evening shortly after their return, the family held a séance for Hubbell. They all sat around a table and heard knockings in response to their questions. Esther said that "Bob" and "Maggie," the ghosts, were both present, and so they were tested. Hubbell asked questions to which nobody, not even he, knew the answers, such as the number on his pocket watch, the date on the coins in his pocket. The rappings told the correct numbers in every case. The actor began to be amazed. He wrote, "I was willing to acknowledge that there might be a power of some kind about the girl, but, of course, nothing supernatural; no ghosts, or such delusions of the imagination." He planned to expose it, "For I had been so successful in exposing alleged 'mediums' in the United States, that I felt it would only be a short time before I should see exactly how she managed to humbug people so successfully as to become the wonder and talk of Canada." So he made arrangements to board with the Teeds during the summer, to be closely at hand to observe . . . and expose.

He had been in the house only a few minutes when his umbrella was thrown across the room (by no visible agent). A few minutes later, as Esther walked out of the pantry with a large dish in both hands, a big carving knife came whizzing through the air, passing closely over her head. It came from the pantry, so Hubbell rushed in to see who threw it—but nobody was there.

"I immediately left the room, taking my satchel with me to the parlor, where I sat down literally paralyzed with astonishment. I had only been seated a moment when my satchel was thrown across the room, and, at the same instant, a large chair came rushing from the opposite side of the room. . . . Just think of it; all while the sun was shining, the birds singing . . . I was a skeptic no longer, but was convinced that there is an invisible power within the atmosphere that men have, so far, failed to comprehend, and that at last it had struck me like a cyclone."

The cyclone continued to blow. Later, as he entered the parlor, seven chairs fell over. He went into the dining room and all the chairs fell over. He began to ask questions and the force rapped on the table in reply. Overcome, Hubbell went into the living room and lay down on the couch, and just then a large glass paper weight, weighing fully a pound, "came whizzing from a corner of the room," some twelve or fifteen feet away, and struck the arm of the sofa, barely missing his head.

"I don't think they like you," said Esther. He wondered if she might not be right.

Whether they liked him or not, they seemed determined to prove to him that they were there, and they were real, whatever they were. After a lull on Sunday, their day of rest and the family's day of restoration, the ghosts began on Monday morning in full vigor, and from then on until later in the summer, Esther became the object of increased persecution. A slap would be heard distinctly by all present and then red finger marks and welts would appear on her face. Hubbell writes, "During an entire day I was kept busy pulling pins out of Esther; they came out of the air from all quarters, and were stuck into all the exposed portions of her person, even her head, and inside her ears."

Deciding to use this force to advantage, and by then—particularly after the episode of the striped stockings—finally convinced it really was ghosts, Hubbell, wanting to light his pipe, said, "Bob, I would like a few matches, if you please."

Instantly matches fell from the air, near the ceiling. After that "I was literally showered with matches; the ghost, Maggie, gave me forty-five during one day, and on another occasion, forty-nine."

During the latter part of July the ghosts became so powerfully demonstrative that it was no longer safe to have Esther in the house. Fires were continually being started; the walls were broken with household furniture; bedclothes were pulled off in the daytime; sofas and tables were turned upside down; knives and forks were thrown with such force that they would stick into doors; foods disappeared from the table; and "worse than all, strange, unnatural voices could be heard in the air, calling us by our names. . . ."

This was too much for the owner of the house who asked the Teed family to leave, in order that his property would not be destroyed. Instead of their all moving, poor Esther had to leave home again. She was welcomed at a Mr. VanAmburgh's farm where she had been before, and where the ghosts hadn't bothered her. After she left, the Teeds and Walter Hubbell walked around their house and called to the ghosts. "Bob, Maggie," they called out. But there was no answer. The ghosts were gone. They had followed Esther.

Hubbell went back to the United States and resumed his acting career, but during the years he kept in touch by letter with the Teeds, and once he returned for a visit to Amherst. By then Esther had left town. He learned that while she was working on the farm of County Clerk Davison, she (or her ghosts) had set fire to the barn.

Esther had been arrested as an incendiary, tried, convicted, and sentenced to four months in jail.

"That judge and jury did not believe in ghosts, and I was not there to explain," wrote Hubbell.

However, he states that her previous good character and virtuous life, and the knowledge of so many of the inhabitants as to the true nature of her ghostly troubles raised a whirlwind of public sentiment in her favor and after being confined for one month, she was released.

Hubbell relates that "Bob, the demon-ghost, was finally scared away from Esther" by the incantations and conjurations of an unidentified "Indian Medicine Man" or "Witch Doctor" and promised never to follow or molest her again. She married twice, and had a son by each marriage. She died in Brockton, Massachusetts, on November 8, 1912, having lived as quiet a life as possible from the moment she left Amherst.

Anyone who's ever been haunted as she had, would very likely think for the rest of her years that combing her hair, or preparing a cup of tea, was enough excitement for the day.

CHAPTER TEN

Poltergeists of the Past

Folklore, fiction, and fraud inevitably prove to be the answer for some cases in every category we might wish to discuss in this book, and they take care of an occasional poltergeist. But some poltergeists produce phenomena which cannot be accounted for in any normal manner. Supernatural explanations are harder to take, but what else is there? Yet when dishes begin to fly and furniture moves of its own accord, it is almost impossible for an individual in our sophisticated era to accept the theory that his home is besieged by a ghost. He will try desperately to find a scientific answer first.

Parapsychologists are the only scientists who yet take the poltergeist seriously. (It's easy for individuals in other disciplines to dismiss as nothing but fraud a case which they haven't bothered to investigate.) Parapsychologists suggest that the unseemly disturbances may be caused by psychokinetic force—the power of the mind over physical objects. As one of them said, "Make no mistake about it, psychical phenomena do exist. Biology will have to revise some of its concepts and admit a force in the human body which can move objects at a distance without muscular contact." This psychokinetic force, he believed, comes from unconscious emotional conflict in the personality of the individual about whom the poltergeist activity centers; and usually in the besieged house researchers do find an unhappy child in puberty or a disturbed older person who has definite personality problems.

Poltergeists have been recorded ever since history began. Efforts to explain them, up until the present scientific era, were simple. They were caused by either one thing or another—either the Devil and his demons or ghosts of departed friends or enemies, trying to make their presence known to prove that they had survived death or trying to revenge themselves on someone who had done them wrong. You could take your choice. Since many poltergeists in the old days were said to talk, the "noisy ghost" definition was probably the more popular; although the Devil had a strong hold on imaginations, too, and was believed capable of producing any hateful phenomenon poltergeist might.

One of the earliest poltergeists to have been written up in detail occurred in 1695 at the home of Andrew Mackie of Ringcroft, England. Alexander Telfair, an observer of the phenomena, wrote a book about what he saw. It was called, for some reason, *A New Confutation of Sadducism,* and was printed by Andrew Bell in 1696. It gives us an excellent report of the day-by-day activities as attested to by several ministers, lords, and other prominent persons. The action started in February, when Mackie discovered one morning that all his cattle had escaped from their shed during the night. The next night the same thing happened, and one of the beasts was found tied up to a high beam in the shed, so that its feet barely touched the ground. Naturally a watch was kept after that for a mischievous neighbor; but soon the pranks got so completely out of hand that no human agency could possibly be credited.

From time to time during the period between February and the end of April the following things occurred: there were stones thrown all over the house; residents were pulled from their beds by an invisible agency; stones and staves beat people and drove them outside. Three witnesses, while at prayer beside a bed, had an experience which one of them described as follows: "I felt something thrusting my arm up, and casting my eyes thitherward perceived a little white hand and an arm, from the elbow down, but it vanished presently."

During family prayers the spirit, as they called it, repeatedly cried, "Hush! hush!" or whistled and groaned. Several times it ignited the house. Once the children coming in "saw something like a person sitting by the fire, with a blanket about it." The youngest, who wasn't scared a bit, ran and pulled the blanket off because it was his and he wanted it. There was nothing under it but a four-foot stool turned upside down.

On April 5th a group of local ministers formed themselves into an exorcizing committee in an attempt to lay the specter, but it threw stones at them. Some witnesses were levitated by something that gripped their legs and feet. On April 26th the bogy spoke, saying it would take them all to hell. It concluded with the words "thou shalt be troubled till Tuesday." Fires were set every day after that. On Tuesday night those in the barn observed a big black thing in the corner which increased gradually in size. It was like a big black cloud. It gripped some individ-

133

uals there by their arms so hard that it bruised them and they were sore for five days after. Its last act was to set fire to the little sheep house, but the sheep were gotten out safely. And then it disappeared, to be heard from no more.

One of the best-known of all poltergeist hauntings was in the home of the Reverend Samuel Wesley, the father of John Wesley, the founder of Methodism. The scene of the activity was the Epworth Rectory in Lincolnshire, England, where the great preacher was born. The manifestations occurred in December and January, 1716–1717, at a time when young John, then thirteen and one-half, was away at school at Charterhouse. The ghostly adventures were reported in a series of letters written by his mother, father, and sisters to Samuel, the rector of Epworth's eldest son, who was away in London.

It was on the first day of December that the maid heard moans. Several nights later strange knockings sounded in divers places in the house, and these continued for a fortnight. There were also clompings as if someone were walking overhead in the attic and running up and down stairs. Once, it sounded as if a bag of money was emptied at Mrs. Wesley's feet, and again as if all the bottles under the stairs were dashed to a thousand pieces. But the bottles were intact, and Mrs. Wesley couldn't buy bread with the invisible pence.

Susannah Wesley wrote, "I heard something walk by my bedside, like a man in a long nightgown." Emilia wrote, "Sister Hetty, [age nineteen,] who sits always to wait on my father going to bed, was still sitting on the lowest step on the garret stairs, the door being shut at her back, when soon after there came down the stairs behind her, something like a man, in a loose nightgown trailing after him, which made her fly rather than run to me in the nursery."

The family began to call this intruder Old Jeffry. Their dog, a mastiff, was more afraid of him than any of the children. John Wesley, writing later about the haunting from the accounts of those who participated in it, said, "It never came once into my father's study, till he talked to it sharply, called it *deaf and dumb devil,* and bid it cease to disturb the innocent children and come to him in his study, if it had anything to say to him . . . I asked my sister Nancy (then about fifteen years old) whether she was not afraid . . . she answered, she was sadly afraid it would speak, when she put out the candle; but she was not at all afraid in the daytime, when it walked after her as she swept the chambers, as it constantly did, and seemed to sweep after her. Only she thought it might have done it *for her,* and saved her the trouble."

The spook manifested itself thrice like a badger, and once like a rabbit. The servants heard it gobbling once like a turkeycock. Robert Brown, the father's servant, saw the handmill whirling about by itself. He said, "Nought vexed me but that it was empty. I thought, if it had been full of malt he might have ground his heart out for me."

From the senior Wesley's diary we read: "When we were at prayers for King George and the Prince, it would make a great noise over our heads constantly." And when this noise was heard, the wind commonly rose and whistled very loud round the house. Emilia reported, by way of resumé, "It continued a month in its full majesty, night and day. Then it intermitted a fortnight or more, and when it began again, it knocked only on nights, and grew less and less troublesome, till at last it went quite away."

It is interesting that poltergeists so frequently seem to have committed their atrocities in the homes of church officials. Someone suggests this is perhaps because after a person dies he discovers that life in the hereafter is nothing like his parson had led him to believe. Then he wishes to take revenge on the one who sold him a false bill of goods. Of course, such an idea is not for me to comment on.

In the United States there were several very interesting poltergeist cases in past centuries. Regarding one of these, the August, 1868, issue of the *Atlantic Monthly* carried an article by H. A. Willis, a sorely troubled man. He was troubled because he had no belief in Satan and his imps, and he had only contempt for Spiritualists, with their silly sponsorship of ghosts. He was a man dedicated whole-heartedly to science, and so when poltergeist activity began with a vengeance in his home, he turned to men of science to investigate it. Even as frequently occurs today, they laughed at him. But he was wisely aware of the importance of careful documentation, and so his account of his experiences is of definite value, especially since it was written almost immediately after the occurrences.

His poltergeist arrived in his home when he employed an Irish maidservant of eighteen, Mary Carrick, who had recently immigrated to the United States. She was a good girl and a hard worker, and seldom left the house because she knew so few people in America. But after six weeks, suddenly the bells hanging in the kitchen, and communicating with the outside doors and the rooms of the house, began ringing for a half hour or longer at a time during the day and evening.

Willis disconnected all the wires, because he thought the rats must be at them, but the bells continued to ring when Mary was in or near the kitchen, even without their connecting wires being attached. Then raps occurred, loud and frequent, all over the house, and even in the girl's room when she was asleep. Chairs were tipped over and crockery thrown about, tables lifted and moved and kitchen utensils hurled here and there. Mary became very nervous and hysterical, and protested that she had no hand in these disturbances, which indeed, she could hardly have caused by herself. "Please don't send me away!" she would beg in tears. "I haven't a friend in America." This was true, for when word of the poltergeist got out, Mary's Irish acquaintances shunned her as one possessed of an evil spirit and probably in league with Satan.

Willis began to keep a diary of events, and the following are some quotations from it:

"On August 5 Mary was washing clothes when a bench, having upon it two large tubs filled with water, was suddenly moved several inches. The lid of a copper wash boiler was repeatedly thrown up when the girl was not near enough to touch it. These occurrences were observed by different members of the family.

"The next day when Mary was ironing, the table at which she worked continually lifted itself, and annoyed her so much that she shifted her work to another table which proceeded to act up in the same way. Her flatiron, which she had left for a moment, was thrown to the floor."

"On the 26th and 27th of August there was hardly a

half hour of peace." Raps banged on the walls. Chairs and other pieces of furniture shoved themselves about. A wash-tub full of clothes in soak was thrown from its bench to the floor and its contents dumped out. A stool with a pail of water on it glided over the floor. A kettle on the sink lifted itself over the side and banged on the floor. In the girl's room the furniture was so active that Willis had every-thing moved out but the bed for the sake of quiet.

Eventually poor Mary suffered a nervous collapse and was sent off to an insane asylum. In three weeks she was back again, calm and happy. Later she had another hysteri-cal attack from which she recovered quickly; but this time she chose to remain happily employed as a maid at the institution. This decision was gratefully received by the harrassed Willis family.

Willis observed that Mary became clairvoyant quite often during the time she was with him. He tells of an occasion when she insisted that a young woman member of the family, who was in a distant city at the time, was sick. Mary was told that the girl had been heard from recently and was perfectly well, but she maintained nonetheless that the girl was ill, suffering great pain from a sore place on her hand. Later it turned out to be exactly as Mary had described.

Because of this fact, it would definitely seem to me that it was Mary's mediumistic talents which made her the focus of the poltergeist activity. Many mediums who are not trained find themselves subjected to unpleasant treat-ment, until they have learned to protect themselves. Being a go-between for two worlds presents many great problems. It is this mediumistic aspect of the phenomena which leads one to consider more carefully the concept that poltergeists really are entities still living after death and endeavoring to make their presence known—and that they use in their efforts the psychokinetic force of a living human being.

Of course, poor Mr. Willis would consider no such possible explanation. He wanted to be strictly scientific all the way. He says that he tried his best to interest two learned professors in one of the educational institutions nearby (probably Harvard) in his situation when it was at its worst, hoping that they might conduct observations and experimentation along scientific lines. But his request was treated with contempt. The professors told him that he was being imposed upon, he was just a credulous fool, that he should look out sharply for trickery. This to Willis, who had been scrutinizing the activity carefully for over two months! He was infuriated—perhaps justifiably.

CHAPTER ELEVEN

Poltergeists in Modern Homes

In 1957 America became poltergeist conscious as never before because of "The House of Flying Objects." The home of James M. Herrmann of Seaford, Long Island, New York, received a great deal of nationwide publicity when bottles blew their screwed-on tops, and dishes, an electric record player, bottles of holy water, and various other paraphernalia took off in apparently self-propelled flight.

The activity at the Herrmanns was violent for several months and then it stopped as abruptly as it began, and no one has ever found an explanation for it—other than this strange word "poltergeist." Of course, we realize that the word is only a *name* for the specific kind of phenomenon—it is not an elucidation. But whether a haunting of this type is explainable or not, it happens often, and it happens in this modern world as frequently as it ever did in the past.

Since the Seaford case, there have been a number of others about which we have read in the newspapers, although we tend to accept them with a certain skepticism because we really don't know what they're all about. There was, for instance, the Indianapolis poltergeist in the home of Mrs. Renate Beck; and the Baltimore poltergeist, which occurred in the home of Edgar G. Jones, who had recently retired after thirty-seven years with the Baltimore Fire Department. His grandson Ted was the focal point of this activity, although no one blamed him for actually throwing things or anything like that. He was old enough and intelligent enough to know better.

Little Susan, the granddaughter of the James Mikuleckys of Rest Haven, Illinois, was afraid at first that she would be blamed for all the foolishness which suddenly occurred when she was visiting her grandparents. But when she tried to leave she couldn't pack because her tooth paste and other objects would not stay in her suitcase. When her mother, who was ironing, was showered by mothballs which dropped from the ceiling, and Susan was hit on the back of the head by a cabbage, there was pretty good evidence that Susan was not, at least consciously, the instigator.

There was the poltergeist in the home of the family of Frances Smyth in Montreal, Quebec, which tied knots in everything in the house. For six weeks the clothes in the wardrobe, the curtains at the windows, the dresser scarfs, bed covers, anything it was possible to tie, would be tied. One night the family came in to find the portieres—large curtains that serve as interior doors—which separated the dinette from the hallway, and the arms of the overcoats of the five teen-age boys in the family, all done up together in one large knot. Jammed into the middle of the tangle was the umbrella from the front hall rack.

When a child in puberty has big problems, his psychokinetic force may be more easily activated, according to parapsychologists. A case known as the "Newark polter-geist" would suggest excellent ground for the possible truth of this theory. There was ample evidence that the little boy involved was not actually throwing the objects which flew in the apartment. They came toward him rather than away from him; and they were observed in flight on occasion by trustworthy witnesses. But of all children, this one would seem to have had the most to cause him frustration, anxiety, and unhappiness.

The siege began on May 6, 1961. It was Ernest's thirteenth birthday. A pepper shaker came floating by and landed beside the startled lad as he was doing his homework.

Then for nearly two weeks the crockery in his grandmother's four-room apartment on the first floor at 125 Rose Street in Newark, New Jersey, was in more or less frequent orbit. There were a number of responsible witnesses to the events that took place in Mrs. Maybelle Clark's home during this time.

The thirteen-year-old Negro boy who was to be the focus of the phenomena was Ernest Rivers. Ernest lived with his grandmother, Mrs. Maybelle Clark, at the Rose Street address. When the phenomenon first began, Mrs. Clark described it only to members of her family and to a few close friends. But such news is bound to leak out and before long Mrs. Clark regretted deeply the resultant publicity and notoriety.

She became more and more reticent. She shunned all reporters. She refused to allow her picture to be taken, although persistent newspaper photographers managed a few anyway. Mrs. Clark didn't let anyone take Ernest's photograph, either. She was afraid people would think both she and the boy were losing their minds. And she had another reason. She lived in the Felix Fuld housing project in Newark and she didn't want the housing authority to feel that she might be an undesirable tenant or involved in a hoax. She had lived in the project for twenty years and valued her reputation.

Apparently she did not have to be worried about these things. Too many people witnessed the spontaneous phenomena not to prove that something beyond trickery was going on. Irving Laskowitz, director of tenant relations of the Newark Housing Authority, investigated the case as soon as it came to his attention. He stated, "We found no evidence of manual participation. I only wish we had; naughty children are much easier to deal with than invisible pranksters."

Mr. Laskowitz thought that perhaps Mrs. Clark and Ernest could leave the poltergeist behind if they moved to another apartment in the building. However, Mrs. Clark, although frightened, was spunky.

"No," she said. "I don't think this is going to go on forever."

Mr. Laskowitz agreed with her. "Pretty soon you'll run out of things to break," he said.

By this time news of the phenomena had spread throughout the neighborhood and the city of Newark. Neighbors were in the house most of the time. Mrs. Cordelia Holland, who lives on the third floor of the building, said, "We were in the kitchen and suddenly I saw this glass decanter on top of the refrigerator start to move toward the edge. I yelled and caught it just in time. I put it

143

back and made sure it was in the middle of the refrigerator top. A half hour later, when we weren't looking, we heard a crash and found the decanter on the floor."

While Mrs. Clark, Ernest, and two women neighbors were in the apartment a jar of petroleum jelly left a shelf in the bathroom, whizzed through the pantry, rounded a corner, and crashed on the living room floor.

One evening as Mrs. Clark and her grandson were eating dinner in the kitchen four cups jumped out of a punch bowl in the living room and crashed to the floor. At other times, a cup skittered from the rear of a pantry shelf and fell to the floor with a crash; a light bulb unscrewed itself from a floor lamp in Ernest's bedroom and shattered; a small mirror and a bottle dropped to the floor in the bedroom; a bottle of disinfectant flipped off a bathroom shelf; a drinking glass left the kitchen sink, swung around the corner to shatter on the living room floor; a teapot lid tumbled off a shelf to crash in pieces on the floor; an ash tray jumped over a Bible lying on a table and landed on the rug below.

One morning Mrs. Clark awakened with a start as a bottle of furniture polish scraped across the floor of her bedroom. As the days wore on her initial fear was almost crowded out by her exasperation at having to spend most of her time picking up broken glass and mopping up the contents of smashed bottles.

On Friday, May 12, the five-pound electric iron sailed into Mrs. Clark's bedroom from its place on the utility shelf in the hall. Its cord was streaming straight out behind it like an overlong tail. Mrs. Clark said she never would have believed her senses if she had been alone but fortunately Mrs. Holland was with her and saw it too.

James Moore, an assistant director of the Newark Housing Authority, was in the apartment a few days later when Ward Ulrich, a reporter from the Newark *Star-Ledger,* was there. Ulrich was standing in a small hall. He heard someone wail as they often did when the bric a brac began to bounce about and wheeled just in time to watch a bottle come down to a neat three-point landing in Mrs. Clark's bedroom. Picking it up, the two men discovered it to be a medicine bottle with a plastic cap. It had been sitting on the hall shelf before its sudden flight. At this time Ernest was standing about a foot inside his own room, according to Ulrich, who doubts that the boy could have thrown the bottle and then jumped to another position before it landed.

Reporter Ulrich questioned witnesses of other incidents, all of whom were convinced that what they had seen was not caused by pranksters. "These witnesses were all rational and normally intelligent people," Ulrich stated. "None of them seemed emotional or hysterical."

The greatest emotional displays came from crowds who gathered outside the apartment building. Every night the streets were patrolled by persons eager to see the "ghost house." Noisy children and sometimes drunk and disorderly adults kept disrupting the peace of the neighborhood. Ernest and his grandmother grew to be more afraid of them than of the poltergeist.

On several nights they sought refuge at the home of Mrs. Clark's daughter, Ruth, and her husband, William Hargwood. This had the added advantage that when Ernest was somewhere else than his home the spook sulked and wouldn't play.

The late Dr. Nandor Fodor discussed this case with me

while I was researching it and was writing an article about it. He believed that this was typical of other cases where psychokinetic action was probably present. The psychological upheaval caused by Ernest's emotional problems, he thought, might certainly be at the bottom of the trouble. Ernest had more reasons for being emotionally upset during his short life than any child could be expected to endure. His life had taken a most tragic turn in 1956 when his mother, Ann Clark Rivers, killed his father, Ernest, a former professional lightweight boxer. Mrs. Rivers said she had dreamed her husband was going to kill her and she shot him before she had fully awakened.

She pleaded guilty to a charge of second-degree manslaughter and was sentenced to from eighteen to twenty-two years in Clinton Reformatory for Women.

In April, 1961, Mrs. Rivers escaped from that minimum security institution and was still at large when the events related took place. Here would seem to be an immediate trigger for an intensifying of emotional problems—and for the poltergeist manifestations that took place a month later.

After his mother was sent to the Reformatory, Ernest went to live with his grandparents. In 1960 his grandfather died. From that time on Mrs. Clark, the grandmother, centered all of her attention on her small grandson.

Yet there were curious omissions in the affections she showered on him. Ernest was a likeable boy and the neighbors say he was very well-behaved. A neighboring baker presented him with a small cake for his thirteenth birthday—but his grandmother gave him no present.

It would seem, therefore, that such events as this set the stage for the drama that Ernest's unconscious personality played out in poltergeist activities—if Dr. Fodor's theories are correct.

Whatever the cause, the Clark apartment was deluged by visitors who wanted to investigate, to help, or to see ghost-ridden saucers fly through the air. Two Rutgers University students came hoping to give Ernest tests for psychokinetic ability. Edward J. DelRosso, a general contractor of Matawan, New York, said he had many years' experience in banishing poltergeists, and obtained permission to exorcise the "ghost." He burned a candle in the Clark living room and stared into a glass of water, which he used for a crystal. DelRosso said, "The spirits of those who have passed away often return to complete unfinished business."

DelRosso was right about one thing—the poltergeist had unfinished business. It returned that night to pitch a small can of paint from that particularly vulnerable shelf in the hall and to toss a vial of antiseptic out of the bathroom medicine cabinet into Mrs. Clark's bedroom.

Through a relative of the Clarks who was employed as a mail boy where Mrs. Wrege worked, Dr. Charles Wrege learned about the poltergeist phenomena. Doctor Wrege was assistant professor of management psychology in the School of Commerce, New York University, and was interested in the psychology of these unusual events. He visited the home a number of times and won the confidence of Mrs. Clark and Ernest. Doctor Wrege stated that on three separate occasions while he was in the apartment with Ernest objects were propelled by an unknown force when the boy himself was obviously in no position to hurl them. Doctor Wrege carefully measured distances and investigated every object in the rooms to make sure no

147

trick was involved. He is convinced that Ernest could have done nothing physical to influence the action of the objects.

On the night of May 13 the crowds outside the apartment house were particularly noisy. They banged on the door and shouted to see "that boy who makes things fly." About 10 o'clock Hargwood came to take his mother-in-law and Ernest home with him. Just then a small ash tray broke itself. Mrs. Clark immediately called Dr. Wrege as she had promised to let him know the next time the poltergeist became active.

When Doctor Wrege arrived at the apartment and saw that they were preparing to move out for the night he asked, "Can't you leave the boy with me? Maybe there will be other manifestations when we are alone in the house."

So Mrs. Clark, almost as shattered as her dish supply by now, left Ernest with Doctor Wrege. The psychologist and the boy settled down to see what would happen. Doctor Wrege had had an unusually busy and active day and Ernest was weary and miserable about all the commotion.

Dr. Nandor Fodor points out that their weariness was probably the reason so much was to happen that night. It is well-known that relaxation makes psychical phenomena more likely to occur among people receptive to it.

They hadn't long to wait.

The two were in the kitchen when they heard a crash from the living room. It was at least twelve feet from where they stood. They rushed in to find a table lamp smashed upon the floor. Wrege knew Ernest hadn't pushed or pulled the lamp because he had been standing beside the boy. However, he carefully checked the remains of the lamp and its cord and plug for any strings or threads or apparatus whereby someone might have pulled it over. He found nothing.

A few minutes later they were back in the kitchen standing a few feet from the drainboard when a glass left it and smashed to bits *in the air* as it fell to the floor.

"An especially odd thing about both those objects," Doctor Wrege says, "was that they shattered as if hit by some very strong force."

The psychologist was intrigued also by the fact that the broken pieces of each object were all the same size.

Just then there was a crash and a thud from Mrs. Clark's bedroom, but they could guess by the milling, shouting crowd outside what they would find there. Someone had thrown a rock through the window.

Ernest had seemed to grow less alarmed at the poltergeist manifestations as they continued day after day, but now he was really frightened by the mob outside. Doctor Wrege called the police and Ernest's Uncle William. All arrived at the same time. The policemen poked around the apartment trying to find out what kind of highjinks were going on. Then, having discovered nothing, they dispersed the crowds and left.

Doctor Wrege, Ernest, and Mr. Hargwood were getting ready to leave when a pepper shaker hit Hargwood on the back. A few moments later a heavy ash tray grazed his chin. The ash tray was put back on its table but shortly thereafter fell to the floor again between the two men. At this time Ernest was not under close observation and, although Wrege did not believe the boy threw these objects, he could not say categorically that he did not.

The next and final incident was a clear-cut case of

poltergeist activity, with no possible excuse to blame it on anything else. Ernest, a thoroughly scared boy, was standing in the hallway preparing to go out the front door. The two men were still in the living room. At that moment the salt cellar came flying in from the kitchen, which is off to the right, opposite the hall where Ernest stood. It hit Hargwood on the head but surprisingly enough did not hurt him. He had not complained of being injured by any of the blows he had received that evening.

And so, frightened by the unknown within and the known without, the three escaped to the Hargwood home. The boy remained with his uncle and aunt for some time; and the poltergeist did not resume its activities in any large way when he returned home.

Here the affair ended. Like most poltergeist cases it started in the air and ended in the air—without any solution.

A small house, called a "villa" in England, in Eland Road, Lavender Hill, Battersea, a bustling working-class district of London, would have few attractions for a poltergeist—one would think. Yet in November and December, 1927, and January, 1928, there were various commotions for a while that seemed to be definitely supernormal in character.

This villa was inhabited by Mr. Henry Robinson, an invalid of eighty-six, who had lived there twenty-five years, and who was removed to the infirmary at the request of the family when the disturbances commenced. With Mr. Robinson senior lived his twenty-seven-year-old son Frederick and his three daughters: Miss Lillah Robinson, Miss Kate Robinson, and Mrs. George Perkins, a widow, who had a fourteen-year-old son, Peter. The Misses Robinson were school teachers and their brother was a tutor.

The house in Eland Road was of a type of which tens of thousands can be found scattered all round the metropolis. It had two floors and a small garden at front and rear, and was the typical abode of the London artisan. From the garden could be seen the back windows of some premises occupied by a medical practitioner who kept a private asylum or mental home, men suffering from shell-shock being his principal patients. From the doctor's windows to the back of the "mystery house," as the press dubbed it, was about eighty yards. It would have been possible for a person standing at the windows of the private asylum to propel, by means of a catapult, small objects such as coins, pieces of coal, etc., with sufficient force to break the windows of the houses in Eland Road.

When you entered this house it was obvious that someone or something had caused considerable damage— broken windows, smashed furniture, and the debris of ornaments were quite evident. Your initial instinct was to think that some of the mental patients out back had taken a dislike to the Robinson house and given it the business; and I guess that was what the family thought at first, also. When things *inside* the house got completely out of hand, they were forced to change their opinions.

"Except for Percy," said Mr. Fred Robinson, "we have lived in the house for twenty-five years, happily and peacefully. Then on November 29th lumps of coal, pieces of soda, and pennies began to fall on the conservatory—a lean-to building at the back of the house.

"It stopped for a few days. It began again early in December. It struck me as being extremely curious at the

151

time that, although the pieces of coal were very small they broke the glass.

"Things became so serious that I decided to call the police. I had no other idea except that some person was throwing things over the garden wall.

"A constable came along, and together we stood in the back garden and kept watch. Pieces of coal and pennies crashed on to the conservatory roof, but we could not trace their flight. One lump of coal hit the constable's helmet. He ran to the garden wall, but there was nobody there.

"On December 19th our washerwoman said she would not work any longer in the house. She came to me in a state of terror and pointed to a heap of redhot cinders in the outhouse. There was no fire near. How could they have got there?

"Again I called a constable, and we decided to watch in the kitchen. Two potatoes were hurled in while we were sitting there.

"It was on Monday that the climax came—at 9 o'clock in the morning—and for an hour the family was terror-stricken. There were loud bangings in all parts of the house. My sister ran to tell the magistrate. The window panel in my father's bedroom was smashed, and as he was in such a state of fear I decided to remove him from the house. I called in a man from the street, and together we carried him from the room. Just as we were taking him out a heavy chest of drawers crashed to the floor in his bedroom.

"Previously my sister had seen the hall stand swaying and had called me. I caught it before it fell, but some strange power seemed to tear it from my hands, and it fell against the stairs, breaking in two parts."

Mr. Bradbury, the man who was called in to help move the old gentleman, confirmed Mr. Fred Robinson's account. He said:

"Mr. Robinson called me to his house, and when I arrived there at about 10 o'clock there were a fishmonger and a greengrocer discussing with him what had happened. I saw several women in the house and they appeared to be very frightened. Mr. Robinson took us up to a bedroom, where he said his father had been sleeping, and showed us an overturned chest of drawers.

"One of the women said that she was afraid to stop in the house, and that she was also afraid to go into her room to pack up her clothing. We went with her into her room, and she told us that she had been awakened by loud bangings on the door, and the crashing of glass. We stayed there until she had packed her bag and then returned to the back bedroom, where Mr. Robinson showed us pennies and coal on the conservatory roof.

"The four of us—all men—were watching these, when suddenly from another bedroom came a great crash and downstairs we heard a woman scream. We ran to the room and there we saw a chest of drawers lying on the floor. It was all very strange, and Mr. Robinson then took us to the kitchen and showed us the damage done there."

Well, guess who the police decided was responsible for all the foolishness? Mr. Fred Robinson. They wanted to examine him at St. John's Hospital, Battersea, and had him out of the house for several days, although they later reported him perfectly normal and let him return home. Of course, his being away made no difference whatever to the poltergeist. It carried on as usual. Mrs. Perkins reported that while he was gone the manifestations had been both violent and varied. Besides the usual arrival of pieces of coal, etc., there had been "great activity amongst the furniture." Chairs, of their own volition "had marched down the hall single file" and three times Mrs. Perkins attempted to lay the table for Saturday's dinner. On each occasion the chairs had piled themselves up on the table making it impossible for the woman to proceed with the preparation of the meal. At the third attempt she went out into the road and asked a police officer who was on duty there to enter the house and examine the "phenomenon" for himself. The stolid London policeman naturally accused Mrs. Perkins of piling up the furniture herself. A London policeman really has imagination!

Mrs. Perkins' sister, Miss Robinson, stated that after her brother had left the house an *attaché* case "flew" from a kitchen chair to the floor; an umbrella sprang from the stand in the hall to the kitchen floor; a cruet crashed to the ground; and the table fell over after it had been prepared for dinner. She continued: "We were so frightened that we went outside. Through the kitchen window we saw all the kitchen chairs fall over. We went upstairs and found stones on the roof. An extraordinary part about it is that the furniture seemed heavy to pick up again."

Three persons appear to have witnessed the alleged spontaneous movement of the furniture: Mrs. Perkins, Miss Robinson, and Peter Perkins, the fourteen-year-old boy who was so frightened—it was stated—that he could hardly be induced to sit on a chair in case it should move. He was afterwards sent to the country to recuperate. There were still some manifestations even after the household had thinned down to nothing but two women, but somehow it wasn't the same thing at all. If people aren't cringing and cowering around and running for the police and getting all excited, poltergeists don't seem to have much fun. Of course, the activity always peters out eventually, anyway—when the supply of human psychokinetic force runs dry. So the Battersea spook did like the rest; it just quietly stopped manifesting one day and was never heard from again.

The most recent case of poltergeist haunting to gain national attention in the United States occurred in Yucaipa, California. It began on December 6, 1965 and lasted nearly a month. The Los Angeles *Times* of that day headlined the story: THUMPS AND BLASTS OF AIR MYSTIFY HOME OWNERS—DOG JUST LEAVES. Of the actual events, they wrote: "Ghostly thumpings and blasts of air in a home here have not only baffled the owners, sheriff's officers, water men, gas men, builders, and at least one college professor, but also scared the dog into moving out.

"Mrs. Billie Cannon, mother of three school-age children, first noticed the strange phenomena Monday morning in the Cannon house at 33843 Fairview Drive near Redlands.

"She said there was a heavy pounding from inside a heavy wall and blasts of air came up from the concrete floor. The house was at it again that evening when Mrs. Cannon and her husband, Kenneth, came home from work.

"Neighbors were curious at first, Mrs. Cannon said, but are keeping their distance now.

"The house generally acts up for an hour or two in the morning and again in the early evening. In one performance, the Cannon poltergeist, if that's what it is, pounded on the wall forty-nine times, bulging it out five inches.

"Air blasts from the floor raised a rug, ruffled Mrs. Cannon's skirts and bulged out a picture window. In a bedroom a cover popped off the gas heater. Ceramic bric-a-brac fell from a wall and shattered.

After the Cannons phoned the sheriff the house was visited by deputies, gas repairmen, a water crew, a county building inspector, a reporter and a geology professor.

"Theories advanced included house slippage, land slippage, nearby water drilling, and ghosts. No explanation was found, however.

"The Cannon's poodle-cocker hid in the bathroom the first two days, but moved in Thursday with a neighbor.

" 'He wouldn't even eat his hamburger,' said Mrs. Cannon. 'And he loves it.'

"The Cannon home is one of numerous four-year-old houses in a tract, but none of the others is similarly haunted.

" 'You get so you have to laugh about it,' said Mrs. Cannon, 'or otherwise it doesn't take too long to go off the deep end.' "

But Mrs. Cannon found it difficult to keep on laughing about the poltergeist and the following day, the *Times* carried this followup:

"Mrs. Billie Cannon said she and her husband and three children were considering moving out temporarily unless the disturbances let up.

" 'The children are afraid to stay in the house,' said Mrs. Cannon, part-time secretary of the Chamber of Commerce. 'We have been offered a temporary place.'

"The mysterious phenomenon appears intermittently, pounding and bulging interior walls and ruffling rugs with blasts of air.

"Edwin K. Robinson, county building inspector, had suspected two nearby well-drilling operations, but gave up this theory when it was learned that one of the projects was the wrong type to cause such results and the other was shut down by the rain.

"An old resident noted that the tract in which the four-year-old house stands is built over what was once farmland, and suggested it might sit above an old well or irrigation pipes.

"A newspaper reporter who witnessed the phenomenon said it sounded like somebody shooting ducks in the hall-way."

Before the thing finally gave up, it had acquired nation-wide interest. It is an Associated Press dispatch in the Daytona Beach (Florida) *News Journal,* dated January 9, 1966, which gives us the concluding message from the Cannons. It reads:

"The bumping, thumping, knocking, wheezing guest of the Kenneth D. Cannon family has worn out his hosts.

" 'Enough is enough,' said an exasperated Mrs. Cannon Sunday, announcing that her husband is putting their new three-bedroom home up for sale.

"Since Dec. 6, the Cannons have been visited by strange thumpings and air blasts along a hallway wall.

"Geologists, technicians and plumbers have been un-able to trace the source of the noises.

" 'A group of spiritualists say there is a spirit trying to get a message through,' said Mrs. Cannon, mother of three. She said the noises frightened the children, scared off the family dog, and attracted sightseers and 'experts' on the supernatural.

" 'He's not getting through to the Cannons,' she added. 'And even if there is a message, we probably wouldn't want to know about it.' "

It isn't every poltergeist who is lucky enough to have a competent investigator nearby, but fortunately for this one, in Los Angeles lives Raymond Bayless, who has been checking on psychical phenomena for years. He was able to visit the Cannon family right while the activity was at its height, and, since he is a friend of mine, he wrote me about his experience. Now, you must know that the greatest achievement for any psychical researcher is actually to hear or see poltergeist phenomena under controlled conditions—that is, when no person is in a position where he or she could possibly have produced it by normal means. And this is what happened to Bayless and his friend Henry Gilroy, who accompanied him, when they received permission to visit the haunted Yucaipa house. They were lucky enough to hit the jackpot! Bayless wrote me:

"We arrived at the Cannon home at approximately 3:35 P.M. on December 11, 1965, but found no one there. However, Raymond Burris, who lives next door, came over and informed us that Mrs. Cannon had gone to town and would be back shortly. He suggested that, in the meantime, we go on into the house and make ourselves at home. He accompanied us and told us of some of his own personal experiences. He said the noise could be heard distinctly next door in his home, and he insisted that his wife had heard the bumps and bangs during the day when the Cannons were not there. We searched the house and photographed it thoroughly, having the place to ourselves for about twenty-five minutes before the family arrived. Then we saw the station wagon pull up into the driveway; and Mrs. Cannon, her three children, and a dentist, Dr. James M. Lockhart—a personal friend of the family's and a good investigator—came into the house via the garage. Two of the children came through the kitchen into the living room where we were seated, and then started toward their respective rooms. First a little girl, Dee, age ten, passed by and into the hall. She was still in the full view of Mr. Gilroy, and he saw that she was not in any way touching the walls or doors, when a most incredible pounding took place, coming from the bedroom area. It consisted of three heavy blows which shook the house. At that time the boy, Billy, age twelve, was in the living room in full view of the two of us. Mrs. Cannon, Dr. Lockhart, and the other child were still in the kitchen, bringing in the groceries and putting them away. There are no entrances to the house other than the front door into the living room and the back door into the kitchen, so no one could have come in secretly to make the noise."

Naturally, a little boy, especially one who is the focal point of poltergeist activity as Billy obviously was, is not going to understand the value of being completely objective about such goings on. So that he will get further attention, he is very likely surreptitiously to throw things or rap on walls or even break some of his mother's best dishes. For this reason, no one was surprised when further knocks of a similar nature sounded after Billy had gone into his bedroom. Dr. Lockhart, in fact, saw him strike a closet door just inside his room, and the sound was similar to the phenomenon heard earlier. But a small boy's being able to reproduce such noises when he wants to does not in the least mitigate the fact that the sounds also occurred when he was not in any possible position to produce them. Remember that both he and his sister were in full view of Bayless and Gilroy the first time the bangings occurred.

And so, with a little boy in Yucaipa, California, who pounds on doors, but whose doors also pound when he is not anywhere near them, we will leave modern poltergeists for the present. But next time you read in the newspaper that a "noisy ghost" has started its activity somewhere in the country, think of me. After all this writing about them I'm so curious to see one in action that I'll probably be rushing off to investigate it personally.